CHOSEN BY GOD

Unmerited & Undeserving Sinners

Picked out , Selected and washed clean for a Divine Purpose

Waltere Asili Koti

Table of Contents

ISBN:978-1-959251-28-6

Any references to historical events, real people, or real places are used fictitiously. Names, characters, and places are products of the author's imagination.

Front cover image by Visionary Book Writers

Book design by Expert Book Writers

Proofreading: Bertha Enow

Printed in the United States of America.

Author: Waltere Asili Koti

First printing edition 2024 Publisher :

KOTI BOOKS, Baltimore, Maryland USA

Visit us at www.walterekoti.com

Other books by this author: The Power of Sex; You are Elected; Fending off Suicidal Thoughts; Handling Changing Emotions

DEDICATION

The pages are dedicated to the widows and orphans in the world but particularly, those in Cameroon. We are currently sponsoring several orphan children in Cameroon, where we provide monthly support for accommodation, tuition, feeding, clothing and medical care. The story of one family stands out: A single young mother died suddenly and left three young children to fend for themselves.

Another died and left four kids and the youngest was six. No mom or Dad. In the Western world, there is a welfare system in place to care for abandoned children but in most other countries, such a system is non-existent. According to a UN report, as of about 2019, Cameroon has about 900,000 displaced persons and of which 51% are children. Without family, children as young as six are on their own. Proceeds from this work will be used to support more orphan children.

The issue of orphanages is global. Currently, the war in Ukraine has left millions of children homeless and abandoned.

Introduction

The biblical doctrine of election or chosen by God, is arguably the most despised doctrinal issue by many people in the world at large, in the church in particular and for good reason. This doctrine hits at the core of human pride and the desire to be in-charge and in control of one's destiny. The very idea that God , from the foundation of creation, sovereignly elected or chose some people to be with Him in heaven for ever and the rest were non-elect, non-chosen, passed over and even rejected, is an affront to the natural person. People would often say something like, "A good God would never do anything like that, would He?" Then again, but wouldn't a just God do justice? I would let you think about that and let it sink in.

While serving as associate pastor in a local church in the Maryland area, I was physically and verbally assaulted for mentioning a word that many in and outside the church find reprehensible. While at a church event some years back, I was having a conversation with a fellow pastor, and somewhere along the line, this forbidden word came up and I presented a biblical defense to him and my fellow pastor was red hot and fuming. We were in a parking lot and he was all up in my face as he could be heard from about a mile away. Next time be careful mentioning the word election or chosen by God in a church bible study because it may certainly get you excommunicated from that local church. This is a highly debated and controversial issue! That the God of the universe would dare to pick certain individuals out of His creation and atoned for their sins but the rest will be sent to hell for ever. That seems unfair wouldn't you think? So it seems, but we will take a closer look!

As we are currently faced with electing a President in this country now and every four years, the candidate for President will be presented with the opportunity to choose or elect a running mate. He or she will be presented with a large number of candidates as potential running mates and these potential running mates lack the ability and power to influence the outcome of the process. The outcome is entirely dependent on the independent and sovereign choice of the candidate for President.

I've Been
Chosen
by God!
How about
You?

The concept of an independent choice exercised by the candidate for president is crucial in understanding election or being chosen by God. The running mate cannot cooperate in any way shape or form and even lacks the ability to do so and cannot influence the outcome of the process. The running mate is a passive participant in the choice being made by the candidate for president. This is fundamentally a question of authority and power between the greater and lesser.

The concept of authority and power between the greater and the lesser is intricately intertwined in the concept of election. In this human analogy, the emphasis is in, simply the greater in authority and power and not necessarily in essence of being. Let's say that someone decides to travel to a foreign country to adopt a one year old baby. The adopter, sovereignly elects or chooses the adoptee out of billions of children in the cosmos into his family. The greater (adopter) exercises authority over the lesser (adoptee) and the lesser lacks ability and or authority to influence or coerce the election or choosing powers of the adopter.

Can anyone imagine a scenario where the adoptee could possibly resist the election powers of the adopter? certainly not! Unless someone else acts on their behalf, the adoptee cannot resist and lacks the desire and ability to do so.

So why then do many find the biblical doctrine of election or being chosen by God so reprehensible? I am perplexed thinking about this but yet I am not. The very idea that we are not in control as much as we think is troubling to many. This is one area where the lesser seeks to exert authority over the greater. The one with no power seeks to exert power over the all powerful one. The human desire to be in control is not new. And from biblical times to present day, humans have found the idea that God looks down from eternity past to eternity future and sovereignly elects or chooses those that will believe in Him to be abominable and reprehensible.

Now, what about those that He passed over? Whose fault is it if they believe not? Your eternal destiny hangs in the balance as you ponder these questions. This may be your first time ever being confronted with these questions but these questions have been debated for as long as humans have occupied the earth. Those that argue that God chooses humans to believe in Him, favor (election) and those that believe humans have the ability and capacity to choose God, independent of any action taken by God, advocate for the free will of man.

These issues are so huge, that churches split over them. At the heart of the reformation, more than five hundred years ago, was the issue of control. On one side was the Roman Catholic Church that advocated that the church and ultimately, man was in control and on the other side was Martin Luther, who split from that same church and passionately advocated that God alone was and is in control and not man or the church.

As we are faced every two or four years with electing or choosing people for public offices, from Mayor, Governor, CongressMan and President, etc, I remind you of a much more important election or choice taking place right now and every day across the globe. God has elected or chosen you to be with Him in heaven forever and is selecting or choosing men , women, children and infants from every nation, tribe and tongue right now as you are reading and you could be an elect or chosen of God.

Chapter 1

Human Complete Inability

The doctrine of human complete inability (HCI) cannot be fully understood and appreciated in a vacuum but has to be fully grasped in the context of election or God choosing a people for Himself. In other words, if someone rejects an election then it is because they also reject HCI. The idea that human beings are completely unwilling and incapable of choosing God is at the heart of understanding election or being chosen. Let's take a closer look at the word, "ability."

Merriam's dictionary defines ability as, " the quality or state of being able." This is a very interesting definition as it ties quality or state to ability. One's ability to act or take any action is directly correlated to their quality and state of being. The quality and state of our being is intrinsically tied to our essence and character. Merriam's dictionary defines, "quality," as "peculiar and essential character." Any action or inaction on our part is dependent on the quality or state of our being and hence our ability.

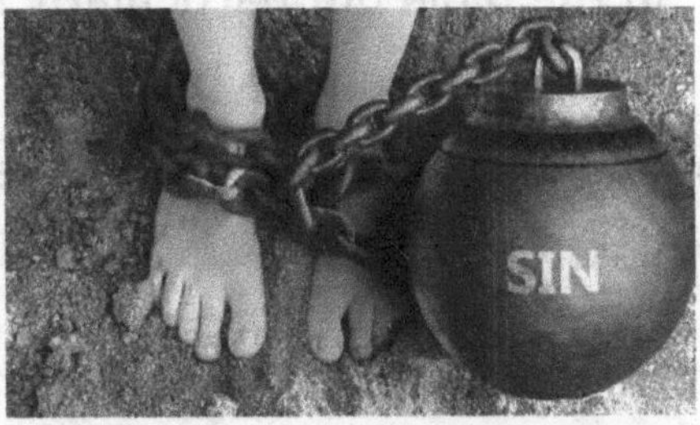

Image of the chains above that bind the human race to sin

The word, "ability" is often translated in the bible as "can," and so when reading the bible and you come across the word "can," you are almost certain that the word should have been better translated as "ability or power." The word translated as "can" has done irreparable damage in almost every sentence in which it is found in the bible.

The word "can" as seen in mostly the New Testament, has been translated from the Greek word, "dunamai," from where we get our English word, dynamite, meaning, powerful explosives. This word is translated in the Thayer lexicon as "to be able, have power." So then when you read the word "can" in the bible but particularly in the New Testament, you are better off reading it as "ability or power."Now, here are some examples!

No one can come to me unless the Father who sent Me draws them, John 6:44. As I have already established the fact that this verse and many like it, should be better translated as, no one has the ability or the power to come to Me unless the Father who sent Me draws or drags them. And so the logical question to ask is why could they not come? And that is a logical and fair question! I have already defined ability as the quality or state of being able. This verse is clearly stating that our lack of ability or power to come is related to the quality of our being which is defined as our peculiar and essential character.

And you who were dead in your trespasses and sins, Ephesians 2:1. This verse clearly states that our deadness which is our essence of being and hence our quality is defective and therefore we possess no ability and or power because we are dead. One of the clearest portraits of human complete inability and hence the quality and state of our being is found in John 11, where Lazarus was dead and was buried and on the fourth day Jesus came and spoke to a dead stinking corpse and he came back to life. This is one of clearest pictures of salvation and complete human inability in all of scripture. Lazarus had no free will to exercise because just as he was physically dead, his freedom of the will was spiritually dead. Only the choosing power of God is able to bring him to life and then God will grant him the desire and ability to exercise his will only after being made alive.

So when Ephesians 2:1 says "you were dead," it is saying that you were dead spiritually just as Lazarus was dead physically. Lacking ability and will to respond to the call of Christ unless God makes sinners alive and compels them to come to him. So then how do some come when John 6:44 clearly states that no one possesses the ability and or power to come? The clue is in the key word in the text, "unless," and that introduces a condition (conditional ability as opposed to absolute ability) that God Himself has to change the quality of the being and infuse in them the ability to come to Him.

This infused ability is necessary and vital to change our natural quality or state of being. *Because the mind set on the flesh is hostile toward God; for it is not subject to the law of God, for it is not even able to do so,*

Romans 8:7. Wow! It is quite interesting that the natural, unsaved person is hostile towards God and even lacks the ability to exercise their will.

The human will can only be exercised within the confines of their ability to exercise such will . The human ability precedes the will and if the ability is lacking, non-existent or disabled then the will is also non-existent. Emmanuel Kant argues against the idea or the concept of moral absolutes. He is quoted as saying that stealing is not a punishable crime if the stealer lacks the ability to control his action at the time of the theft.

" Kant holds the view that in order for this man's action to be morally wrong, it must have been within his control and ability in the sense that it was within his power at the time not to have committed the theft." Kant may be correct in arriving at the conclusion that humans lack the ability to stop a moral conduct from coming to fruition but wrong on the fact that humans cannot be held morally responsible because of the deficiency in their ability to stop such immoral actions.

Kant concludes that, "Moral rightness and wrongness apply only to free agents who can control their actions and have it in their power, at the time of their actions, either to act rightly or not." The implication of Kant's assertion is that humans possess the ability to choose or elect what-ever action they initiate and the power of initiation is within the human. The final implication for Kant is that humans possess the power and ability to elect or choose God for salvation. Just as with the case of Lazarus, a dead corpse lacks freedom and we are born and are by nature dead corpses.

Objections to Human Complete Inability

Those that object to human complete inability will by implication reject the biblical doctrine of election or God's choosing power and will also espouse an alternate understanding of "ability, "and the state of our natural being. Let's examine a bible verse that is often used to advocate for human ability. "*For God so loved the world that He gave His only begotten son, that whosoever believes in Him should not perish but have everlasting life,* " John 3:16. This is arguably the most quoted verse in the bible, even among non-Christians but this verse is widely misunderstood, even among professing Christians.

This verse simply states that the one who believes has everlasting life but makes no mention if the one who believes possesses the ability to exercise their faith to believe. Proponents of human ability would have to import assumed ability into the text to draw that conclusion. "What does this famous verse teach about a fallen man's ability to choose Christ? The answer, simply is. nothing,[1] R.C. Sproul.

The most important words in this passage are "believe" and "everlasting life" but many, unfortunately, have made this verse to be about, "whosoever." This word, "whosoever," has been tied to human ability but this word, simply also means, "whoever," "any- one who," as translated from the Greek and has nothing to do with the ability to believe. The only ones that will believe and have everlasting life are those that have been given to Christ by the Father, John 6:37-39. Therefore the word , "whosoever," does not in any way address the ability to believe of those that will believe but only says that the believing ones were enabled by God to do so.

---

1 https://www.ligonier.org/blog/mans-ability-choose-god/

Another verse that proponents for human ability to elect or choose Christ is, "Choose you this day whom you will serve; whether the gods which your fathers served that were on the other side of the flood, or the gods of Amorites, in whose land you dwell," Joshua 24:15. Proponents for human ability would infer that, Joshua's audience, possesses the ability to obey the command to "choose or elect" whom they would serve. This is what I will call, implied ability as opposed to expressed ability.

The plain reading of the text in no way assumes the ability to choose whom they would serve but today's readers of the text would have to assume that Joshua would not have given a command if his audience lacked the ability, either to obey or to reject the command. The bible is filled with such commands that will leave readers with implied or assumed ability to obey.

The Apostle Paul speaking to the Philippian Jailer, said, "Believe in the Lord Jesus, and you will be saved," Acts 16:31. This verse in no way implies or expresses that the audience possesses the ability to "believe," and we know from other texts that even the ability to believe is a gift. "For it has been granted to you on behalf of Christ not only to believe in Him but also to suffer for Him," Philippians 1:29. Therefore human ability is a function of the human essence and humans cannot exercise any ability from a corrupt nature towards a holy God since any such ability, also is a function of the human will and that will is in bondage to sin.

Chapter 2

Human Will in Bondage

The question often arises, how can a sinful and corrupt human being choose a holy God? The fundamental question is the state of the human will! Is it free or is it in bondage to sin? Those that advocate for human ability would also of necessity see the human will as free and possesses the ability to exercise their will towards a holy God for salvation while those that believe that the human will is in bondage and captive to sin and incapable of exercising their will, unless it pleases a holy God to grant such ability to that undeserving sinner.

At the heart of the doctrine of election or being chosen by God, is the question of the human will, and is it in bondage or is it free? In an article published in Encyclopedia

Britannica, "Free will" in humans is defined as, "the power or capacity to choose among alternatives or to act in certain situations independently of natural, social, or divine restraints."[2]

This secular definition of the "freedom of the human will" has contributed to further damage the gospel message like no other issue. The idea of "freedom of the will and independence of the human will" feeds the natural human tendencies for autonomy from any divine constraints or restraints. It is no surprise that the "freedom of the will" is more appealing than the "bondage of the will" since the freedom of the will puts natural man in control and the bondage puts God in control. And natural man will never willingly tolerate any such encroachment on our much cherished freedom.

---

2 https://www.britannica.com/topic/free-will

This definition also infers that the natural human will, possess, "the power or capacity to choose among alternatives," thus, declaring the human will to be autonomous of any divine constraints. The implication here is that the human will is self sustaining and self governing and has the ability to elect or choose whatever action it conceives. Another implication is that the human will has the ability to act because it cannot elect or choose any activity unless it possesses the ability to do so. The sinner in his or her natural state possesses no such ability because the human will is in bondage to sin and not free as some would have us believe.

One of those who would have us believe that the human will is free, Jacob Arminius, who is a well known and famous proponent of human free will doctrine. In an entry in Wikipedia, he argued that, "Man has a free will to respond or resist. Free will is granted and limited by God's sovereignty, but God's sovereignty allows all men the choice to accept the Gospel of Jesus through faith, simultaneously allowing all men to resist."[3] Arminius infers in his theological understanding of human will that it is free and he would have to assume that the human will is endowed and naturally equipped with the ability to exercise that freedom. Where there is no ability then there is no will and if the ability is disabled or inactive then the will is also disabled and inactive. The will is dependent on the ability.

---

3 https://en.wikipedia.org/wiki/Arminianism

Image of the human will held captive by sin

The position of human freedom stands in direct opposition to Jesus' words, "No man can come to me, except the Father which hath sent me draws him, and I will raise him up at the last day," John 6:44. This verse and many like it clearly states that without divine enablement, humans lack the ability to exercise their will because the will is in bondage to sin, depraved and corrupt .

In Martin Luther's response to Desiderius Erasmus's book, "the freedom of the will," Luther argued that, "sin incapacitates human beings from working out their salvation, and that they are completely incapable of bringing themselves to God. As such, there is no free will for humanity."[4]

Proponents of the freedom of the will have to deny or redefine several core Christian doctrines to allow the freedom of the will any standing. Among them, are the doctrines of election, complete depravity of the human race, predestination and the foreknowledge of God. And chief among these is the complete depravity of the human race. If someone is wrong on this then their entire soteriological framework (ordo salutis) will be called into question.

So when it says in Genesis 2:17 that, "For in the day that you eat of it, you shall surely die," or Ephesians 2:1, that says, "And you

4 https://en.wikipedia.org/wiki/On_the_Bondage_of_the_Will

were dead in your trespasses and sins." The debate between the freedom of the will and bondage of the will hangs on the extent of the fall in genesis 3. This is the Croix of the argument. And we can conclude from the context that, "dead," means spiritual separation between God and Man.

How dead was Adam and by extension, the human race after the fall? partially dead? half dead? completely dead? Is there any such thing as degrees of deadness? How much of the human will was affected by the fall? The ability to exercise the will as it relates to choosing God is proof of life. There is no freedom of the will if humans are spiritually separated from God and the entire human being is dead including their will. The freedom of the will has to assume that the God of the universe is somehow clueless about His creation and does not know who will exercise their free will and He even lacks the ability to have that knowledge.

Chapter 3

God Foreknows You

At the center of God's foreknowledge of you, is the doctrine of election or being chosen by God. Without which, the election crumbles under its own weight. At issue here is divine foreknowledge as the “Divine” is the only being capable of foreknowing and causing future events. Only a being with inerrant and infallible foreknowledge has the ability to cause events that are not yet to come to being.

In an article, titled, "Foreknowledge and Free Will", the author said that, "Theological fatalism is the thesis that infallible foreknowledge of a human act makes the act necessary and hence un-free. If there is a being who knows the entire future infallibly, then no human is free."[5]

---

[5] https://plato.stanford.edu/entries/free-will-foreknowledge/

The author of this article, not necessarily a proponent of divine foreknowledge, but made a philosophical argument that if any being exists that possesses infallible knowledge of any future human acts, then no human is free. It is interesting that this author did not even address the issue of causation of the future act but asserts that a simple foreknowledge of that act renders any future human act un-free.

The word, "foreknowledge," simply means to possess infallible and inerrant knowledge of any future act before that act ever comes to fruition. Free is defined by Thayer's Greek lexicon as, " unrestrained, not bound by an obligation,"[6] and this definition carries the idea of acting independently without any outside influence. The question before us is, can infallible and inerrant foreknowledge and complete human freedom coexist? If God infallibly and in-errantly foreknows those that will believe in Him for salvation

---

6 https://biblehub.com/thayers/1658.htm

and they all actually come to believe, then in actuality, they were not free. Because "any free being" by definition, is unrestrained and not bound by an obligation. Remember the quote by the philosopher, "if there is a being who knows the entire future infallibly, then no human is free." This philosopher made a hypothetical assertion but we know without a doubt that such a being certainly exists. The observation here is that by simply foreknowing any future event, then the objects of that foreknowledge are rendered incapable of acting outside of that foreknowledge and are unable to exercise their free will outside the foreknowledge of the subject. For the human will to be truly free , "meaning independent of God," God must be incapable of foreknowing in potential human action and decisions, else, humans are not free. For the actions of any being to be free, those actions cannot be known by some other being, else that being is not free. The very idea of freedom demands an autonomous will that is not constrained by other beings.

Image of God's Foreknowledge

The biblical idea of foreknowledge also implies an intimate relationship. So when the subject foreknows the object, then, embedded in that foreknowledge, is a relational aspect. This foreknowledge transcends knowing what future actions a being will commit and actually include a love relationship. The idea of God selecting or choosing you is embedded in Him foreknowing you. The Greek word, "*proginosko*" is the word that is translated in our bibles as *foreknowledge* . This is a compound word that stems from two words, "*pro*" and "*ginosko*" . The former word means *before* and latter means, *to know* and hence the definition, know beforehand.

So when the bible says, *And this is eternal life that you may know the only true God,* John 17:3. This text explains that knowing God is eternal life. What in the world is that supposed to mean? Even a layperson can easily read from the context what it is not saying! It is clearly not saying that knowing cognitively is eternal life because even the devil knows God cognitively. This Greek word, *"ginosko"* carries with it a relational aspect and cognitive aspect and the context of its usage will be our guide. This verse is heavily tilted towards the relational aspect without completely discounting the cognitive angle. But when *"proginosko"* is used and God is the subject, which is almost always the case, then that foreknowledge is almost always relational in nature and not cognitive.

Therefore, God, foreknowing you has little to do with the cognitive aspect of foreknowledge. God, frankly foreknows every soul that has ever been born in the cognitive sense but He does not foreknow everyone relationally. If God was to foreknow everyone relationally, then that would be universalism, which simply means, everyone will be saved and are going to heaven and any serious bible student will agree that the bible does not teach that. The bible says that, For those whom He foreknew, Romans 8:29. This verse is clearly teaching restraint and relational foreknowledge. God could have said, the world whom He foreknew but He chose to say, "those whom," meaning a limited or restraint number of people. And since He elected you to be with him forever then, it is logical to see that He will only elect or choose those that He already had a relationship with, (foreknowledge) and those are the same ones that He predestined.

Chapter 4

God Predestined You

God's predestination of you is arguably, the most comforting news out of the bible for many but for many others, this is the most disgusting news. But why this dichotomy? The primary issue here is control and simply, put who is in control. God or man? The very thought of the idea that the destiny of man has been predetermined by God is reprehensible to natural man because our pride and sinful state will never entertain such an idea. Of course, what normal and rational thinking person would cede their destiny to someone else? We are in a free society, right? And no one dare cede their much cherished freedom to some other being, right? Doing that would portray us weak and feeble, wouldn't you think so?

The Power of God in Predestination

Predestination and its sibling, election are amongst the most beloved or the most hated biblical doctrines. Those that love it, do so passionately and those that hate it, do so likewise. The easiest way to split a church is to mention the word predestination and you quickly find out that, about one third of church members would be in support and about two third would oppose it. As a result, most pastors dance around these topics and seldom dig deep into them, leaving their congregants confused and defeated.

The simplest way to explain predestination is that God has sovereignly determined before -hand the destiny of those that will be saved and spend eternity with Him in heaven. This definition, if truly believed, has far reaching implications that will overwhelm anyone's theological system. Your understanding of the doctrine of sin and salvation will be radically altered if by God's mercy, you come to the understanding that God predestined you to believe in Him. Your spirit and soul will be overwhelmed with a deep sense of gratitude and your life will be radically transformed forever.

The word, predestination in the bible is translated from the Greek word, prooizo. Thayer's lexicon defines this word as, *to predetermine, to decide beforehand, to foreordain, to appoint* and when God is the subject, it also means, decreeing from eternity past. [7] This definition lines up perfectly with what I have already established about God foreknowing you and setting you apart from everyone else but for Himself. The key concept in predestination is control and fundamentally, who is in control? God or man?

In an article titled, *Why Losing Control can Make You Happier,* the author RaJ Raghunathgan PhD and a professor of Psychology at University of Texas McCombs School of Business, cited a study that showed that people are less happy when in control and here is the study:

Control also feels good because it makes us believe that we aren't under someone else's control. In one study of an old-age home researchers gave members of one group control over which plant to grow in their room and which movies to watch. The other

[7] https://biblehub.com/thayers/4309.htm

group was denied that control. In the eighteen-month that followed, the death rate of the second group was double that of the first. [8]

The group that was not in control had better health outcomes than the one that was not and ceding control to an outside entity is not logical to the natural man. We are naturally wired to be results oriented and those inputs determine outcomes and anything contrary, is readily rejected and found to be reprehensible by natural man. That is the free will doctrine which is widely and readily embraced because it fits perfectly with our naturalistic inclinations.

But the doctrines of election, divine sovereignty and predestination are almost always readily rejected and found to be reprehensible by natural man. Natural man is declared to be impotent before a potent

---

8 https://greatergood.berkeley.edu/article/item/why_losing_control_make_you_happier

and indomitable God and that cuts to the core of human pride. It will take a radical transformation of the human heart for anyone to embrace these facts and if you have truly come to believe in Jesus Christ for your salvation then that could only have been possible because God predestined you to believe.

For those who God foreknew ,He also predestined to be conformed to the image of His son, Romans 8:29. We can clearly deduce from this verse that those whom He predestined are also foreknown by God either simultaneously or contemporaneously. The relationship between God's foreknowledge and predestination are clearly intertwined and His predestination has its foundation and it is dependent on His foreknowledge.

Therefore, God's predestination of you is among the most exciting and comforting news from the bible. Exciting because it is at the heart of the gospel and whenever I reflect on this truth that God selected me or you from all the billions of people that would ever inhabit the earth to be conformed to His image, that's exciting. This is also comforting in the fact that I am not in control. Thank God I am not in control because if I was, things would be all screwed up. The news keeps getting even better in that He did not only predestinate you but He also called you.

Chapter 5

God Called You

God called you is a phrase that leaves some readers in total consternation and perplexed. This phrase draws the reader into a deep sense of awe and to ponder the depth and breadth of the call of God. But what does it really mean that God called you? In the general sense, a *call is a cry made as a summon or to attract someone's attention.* [9] Meaning to call someone's name or attention towards your direction but, a calling on the other hand, takes a somewhat different meaning. *A strong inner impulse towards a particular course of action especially when accompanied by conviction of divine influence.* [10] A calling is often understood to carry the meaning of a sense of purpose and meaning in life. Some

---

9 https://www.dictionary.com/browse/call

10 https://www.merriam-webster.com/dictionary/calling

one's devotion to a singular course and purpose would exemplify their calling. Albert Einstein's calling was to be a physicist, would be an example of that, So then what does it mean that God called you?

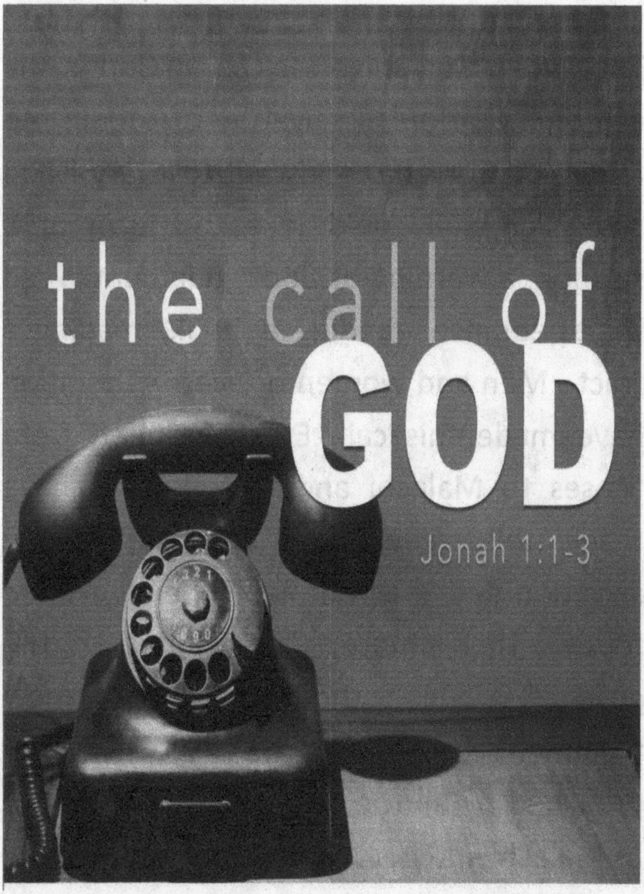
the call of
GOD
Jonah 1:1-3

The term , "call," is often used in two general categories in the bible, a general or universal and a special or effective, efficacious call as is often referred to by most theologians .

The General or Universal Call

The general or universal call of God is the call or invitation to salvation or to join the family of God that goes out to every living soul. This call could take the form of a sermon, a warning of God's judgment, a call to repentance, reading a book, reading a tract . Men and women of every generation have made this call. Every Prophet, from Moses to Malachi and the Apostles have made this general or universal call to salvation and that call is still being echoed today. The phrase, "preaching of the gospel," is widely thought of to be a new testament concept, but the gospel had been preached by all the prophets, from Genesis to Malachi and here are a few examples:

Noah made this call to his generation before the flood waters came and wiped that generation except Noah and his household. And God said, I will destroy man whom I have created from the face of the earth, both man and beast, Genesis 6:7. Noah is ultimately referred to as a preacher of righteousness , 2 Peter 2:5. Noah's building of the ark was in a sense making a general or universal proclamation to his generation of approaching judgment by God.

The ark was large and very visible to all but he was probably mocked and ridiculed for building a vessel that large on dry ground believing that it will rain and the vessel will be lifted up from its base. The news of this boat being built must have spread far enough that everyone came to see the vessel and in so doing , made everyone without excuse.

This was so important that Jesus referenced it as a picture of His second coming, For as in the days that were before the flood, they were eating and drinking, marrying and giving in marriage, until the day that Noah entered the ark, Matthew, 24:38. This is likened to the coming of the Son of Man in clouds of glory, people will be engaged in normal life events and daily activities and without any warning, then it is all over and the end of all things has come. Just as it was in Noah's days, only a remnant was spared (eight people out of millions on the earth at that time) and so this generation will not be spared. No one repented at the preaching of Noah but him and his family and Jesus is telling us to look to that event and have a glimpse of what is coming? really? fall on your face while you have time and turn from your wicked ways while it is day for the knight is coming and it will be dark and too late.

Moses made the general call to his generation, as he said, Moreover, the LORD your God will circumcise your heart and the hearts of your descendants, to love the LORD your God with all your heart and with all your soul, so that you may live, Deuteronomy 30:6. Moses had foreshadowed a message that the rest of the prophets will echo to generation , most notably, Ezekiel and Jeremiah.

Ezekiel made this observation to his generation, A new heart also will I give you, and a new spirit will I put within you: and I will take away the stony heart out of your flesh, and I will give you a heart of flesh. And I will put My spirit within you, and cause you to walk in My statutes, and you shall keep My judgments, and do them, Ezekiel 36:26-27. The issue of the human heart is central to the gospel call because if the heart is cleansed, then the whole body is clean.

Jeremiah proclaimed to his generation what the LORD dictated to him, "For this is the covenant that I will make with the house of

Israel after those days," declares the LORD: "I will put My law within them, and I will write it on their hearts. And I will be their God, and they shall be My people," Jeremiah 31: 33. And at the end of verse 34, it says, "For I will forgive their iniquity, and I will remember their sin no more."

The general and universal call to repentance has been made throughout the old and new testament and is being made today in your hearing. This call is being made today through unlimited media, like radio, satellite, internet, the bible, sermons, tracts. The last 100 years have witnessed the invention of radio, satellite and most recently, the internet to hasten the end of all things as we know it.

God has used men to invent these tools to advance His kingdom agenda in these last days. Everyone will hear this universal call so that all will be without excuse. Everyone in the most remote place on the planet has a phone with internet access and in essence, all peoples will hear the global call to repentance and when all have heard then the end will come. And here is what Jesus said through Matthew, *And this gospel of the kingdom shall be preached in all the world for a witness unto all nations; and then shall the end come,* Matthew 24:14.

Technological advancement will aid usher in the end of all things as we know it. These advancements will be the tools to aid in the rapid fulfillment of Matthew 24:14. The general call to repentance is being made now like no other time in human history. Many more people are now being reached with the gospel without having to travel on horse backs as was then the case. But this general call only serves as a warning to mankind to repent and turn from sin to God. This call is a means to salvation since no one gets saved apart from hearing the word preached and here is what the Apostle Paul said, *For whosoever shall call upon the name of the Lord shall be saved. How then shall they call on Him in whom they have not believed? and how shall they believe in Him of whom they have not heard? and how shall they hear without a preacher?* Romans 10:13-14. Paul is basically laying the groundwork of how the general call leads to another kind of call.

The Special or efficacious call

As the preacher preaches the word (general call), some believe and those that believe are the ones who will call on Him (special call). Believing in God precedes this call because they can only call after they have believed. No one is able to make that call unless they have already believed in God and in other words, calling on God is evidence that they have believed. This effectual, special or efficacious call can be identified in two primary forms: a call to salvation and call to service.

call to Salvation

After an interaction with God's word through preaching or any other medium, the sinner is confronted with a call to repentance (general call), the Holy Spirit will convict the world concerning sin and righteousness and judgment, John 16:8. Only those that God had elected are granted the ability to hear this special call and even dare to respond or answer the call. The rest are unwilling and unable even to hear and let alone, answer the call. This is how Jesus puts it, *He who is of God hears the words of God; for this reason you do not hear them, because you are not of God,* John 8:47.

This call to salvation is a part and parcel of the fact that God elected you for salvation from the foundation of the world to believe. Paul said , Just as He chose us in Him before the foundation of the world, that we should be holy and blameless before Him in love,

Ephesians:14. The word, "chose", used by Paul through the inspiration of the holy spirit, is the same word, "elect", that is at heart of the thesis of this book. Paul dealt with the fact that some were elected but he also dealt with the time of that election and the purpose thereof.

The word, "before," is a clear reference to the time of that election and the word ,"that," introduces the purpose, which is, "to be holy and blameless."This call can only be answered by those that God had elected from the foundation of the world . The story of Jesus raising Lazarus in John 11 is well remembered by many but most people do not bother to consider the spiritual message behind the raising of Lazarus, and as a result, most have no clue. The raising of Lazarus is arguably the most vivid picture of the special call to salvation presented in all of scripture.

Here, we are presented with evidence of a man who was sick and died suddenly and was buried, and was in grave for four days when Jesus arrived. Jesus was told of his illness but Jesus purposely lingered around and even when he died, Jesus did not come immediately but took His time. If He had come immediately after his death, then some would have said something like, he did not really die but was in a coma of some sort. Thanatologists have concluded that after three days, a body in the grave begins to decompose and so Jesus arrived on the fourth day to possibly dispel any notion in the minds of dissenters that Lazarus was not dead but was in a coma.

Lazarus being dead and decaying is the most vivid picture of human total depravity and total inability ever presented in scripture. There is no room to argue for partial deadness and human free will as many have espoused. This man is dead and there is no life in him and any possibility of him exercising his free will has been completely eradicated and extinguished. This is an astounding portrait of the spiritual condition of the human race from the fall of man in Genesis 3 until the return of Christ at His second advent.

All human beings are physically alive but spiritually dead, just as Lazarus was physically dead, so all humans , prior to salvation are spiritually dead. Jesus made this profound call in John's gospel, calling a physically dead person to physical life again, as He said: He cried out with a loud voice, "Lazarus, come forth," John 11:43. The man who had died came forth, bound hand and foot with wrappings, and his face was wrapped around with a cloth. Jesus said to them, "Unbind him, and let him go," John 11:44.

This is a special call to salvation, whereby God Himself calls the spiritually dead to the newness of life in Christ. God calls the dead and He also grants the dead the ability to answer His call. God made Lazarus alive before he could answer His call and in like manner, the elect or those chosen by God can only answer the Divine call after they have been made alive. This is a Divine summon and all that are summoned will respond. When a judge summons you to appear in court, I bet, you do not exercise your free will to decide, if you will appear or not and so is the Divine summon. For some, this special call to salvation is simultaneously intertwined with a call to service .

Call to Service

A call to service, in all likelihood, happens contemporaneously with a call to salvation. Some are called to service at the moment of salvation, and God Himself, places a burden on the life of that individual to do a special work to advance God's program of salvation. This burden is so heavy that such individuals are unable to un-call themselves. Such persons do not even consider their lives worth saving in place of denying the call of God.

The Apostles Peter and John, were admonished to deny their calling and here is that admonishment: *And when they summoned them, they commanded them not to speak or teach in the name of Jesus,* Acts 4:18. And Peter and John responded vehemently: *Whether it is right in the sight of God to listen to you rather than God, make your own judgment, for we cannot stop speaking about what we have seen and heard,* Acts 4:19-20. Peter and John were such persons ,having a deep and profound clarity of mission and purpose to fulfill the burden placed on them and nothing was able to deter them from that call. For some, a call to salvation, often imperatively, accompanies a call to service.

Jeremiah was divinely summoned by God to fulfill a divine assignment. His call to salvation and service were simultaneous and interestingly, these calls happened prior to his birth and here is Jeremiah's account: *Before I formed you in the womb I knew you, And before you were born I consecrated you; I have appointed you as a prophet to the nations,* Jeremiah 1:5. This is one of the most explicit calls to salvation and service in the scriptures. The first part of the verse deals with a call to salvation as he was saved and set apart while in the womb and not yet born and his call to service also happened while in the womb and not yet born, as God appointed him as prophet to the nations. His purpose and mission was clear and not by any means ambiguous. He clearly knew his call and he executed it faithfully and without reservation.

Another old testament prophet that experienced a simultaneous call to salvation and service is Isaiah and here is his account: *Then one of the seraphim flew to me, carrying a burning coal in his hand that he had taken from the altar with tongs. He touched my mouth and said, "Look! Now that this touched your lips, your guilt is taken away, and your sins atoned for."* Isaiah 6:6-7.

Then I hear the voice of the LORD as He was asking, "whom will I send? Who will go for us?" Isaiah 6:8a.

"Here I am!" I replied. "Send me," Isaiah 6:8b.

"Go!" He responded, "Tell this people: Isaiah 6:9a.

Isaiah's call to salvation is clearly elaborated in verse 7 as his guilt was taken away and immediately following that, was a call to service as God made the call in verse 8, when He said, "Whom shall I send? Who will go for us? and Isaiah answered the call by responding, "here I am, send me."

Based on these two accounts of the calls of Isaiah and Jeremiah, and consistent biblical teaching, it is safe to conclude and infer that a genuine call to salvation will also have a simultaneous call to service. I am yet to find an instance in the biblical record where someone is genuinely saved but has no interest in advancing God's plan for salvation for the human race.

Remember the words that the LORD spoke to Pharaoh through Moses, *Let my people go, so that they may serve me*, Exodus 8:1. The reason that God's people had to be let go is for service. If you are saved today, then you have been spiritually taken out of Egypt for service. Remember, you and I are saved for service. The linkage between salvation and service is woven through pages of scripture from Genesis to revelation but no one can genuinely serve unless they have been truly regenerated and justified.

Chapter 6

God Justified You

God justified you or me, is also one of the most comforting messages in all of scripture. This is comforting in the sense that it is completely an act of God and you and are passive participants in God's action of justification. I know by now you may be scratching your head and mumbling within you, what the hell is justification? I am so happy that you dared to ask because, honestly speaking, you are not alone. Justification is central to the Christian faith but many people attend churches for decades and can hardly articulate the fundamentals of this pivotal doctrine.

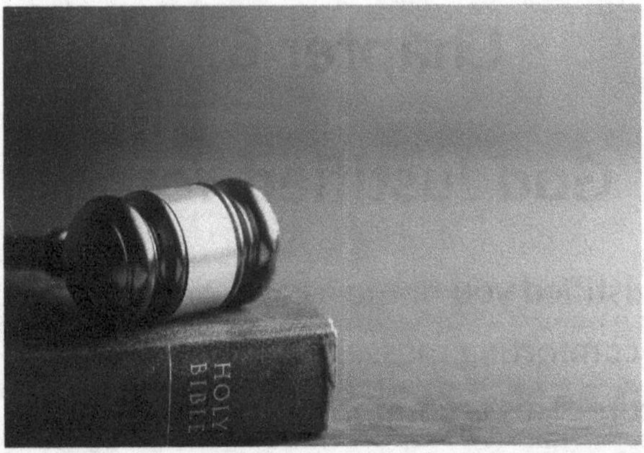

Image of the legal act of Justification

The idea of justification is so central to the Christian faith that churches split over it. We may never have had the protestant churches today if not for the battle over the doctrine of justification. Up to the 1500's A.D , the Roman church was unquestionably the only church in existence globally, and the question of justification arose within that church. Reformers like Martin Luther, John Calvin and others, challenged the Roman church on this question and that ultimately led to the church split and the birth of Protestantism.

This matter was so central to the reformation movement that they coined the phrase, "justification by faith alone." People fought and died for, "justification by faith alone." The word , "alone," was intentionally included to lay emphasis on the exclusiveness of justification to achieving a right standing with God. They emphasized the fact that there are not multiple avenues to get right with God but only one and one alone. That question is still being debated till this very day: How can a sinful human come into a right standing with God?

This is the question of justification. This word simply means to declare a guilty person not guilty of all the charges, to set free, to declare righteous. Thayer's Lexicon defines this word as: to render righteous, to declare just, to declare guiltless, acquitted of a charge or reproach.[11] A person that was formerly a sinner has now been declared a

---

11 https://biblehub.com/thayers/1344.htm

saint and it is completely and totally a work of God accomplished through the shed blood of Jesus Christ. There are three aspects of justification that this chapter will seek to answer or expound on, namely: the act, the means and the result of justification. *Therefore, having been justified by faith, we have peace with God through our LORD Jesus Christ*, Romans 5:1.

The Act of Justification

The phrase, "therefore, having been justified," that appears in the beginning of Romans 5:1 deals with the act of justification, meaning, someone did the work of justifying you and the question is, who? that phrase takes the reader back to the entire chapter 4 of Romans, where the Apostle Paul argued that Abraham was justified by faith and not by works. Whose action justified Abraham? The act of justification cannot be properly grasped without totally embracing the doctrine of election.

Justification has been established as, to mean, declaring a guilty person acquitted of all charges, setting a sinner free from the penalty and ultimately, the presence of sin. If this is true then someone besides the sinner is making that declaration. Let's assume for a moment that the sinners were to make such a not- guilty declaration upon themselves, then such a declaration would be null and void because the sinner lacks the power and authority to make such a declaration.

This will be like Donald J Trump is the Judge in his own impeachment trial or a Judge was charged with murder by the District Attorney and the same Judge was presiding over his own case and I hope the public will not expect a just and fair outcome. Judges are required to be ethical, equitable, fair and impartial and so the notion that the guilty party is also the presiding judge will not make the process ethical, equitable, fair and impartial.

The phrase, *having been justified* , mentioned in Romans 5:1, implies that someone else is performing the act of justification but who is that? The word *justified*, is a translation from the Greek word, *"dikaiothentes".* In the Greek language terms, this word is a participle in the aorist mood and in the passive voice. At this point, you may be scratching your head and thinking, but why do L have to know this linguistic detail? I am very happy you dare to ask! Understanding this detail is extremely critical in determining that someone else justified the elect.

The aorist mood of this word indicates past action,(similar to past tense in English grammar), meaning that your justification happened long before you were even born and the participle indicates that the result of that past action is ongoing. This word is also in the passive voice, simply meaning that someone else is doing the action of justification. If I say that I am driving to New York, simply means that I (the subject) is doing the action (driving) but if I am being driven to New York, simply means that I (the subject) is passive in the action (driving) and some other party is doing the driving and I am passive in the act or a passenger.

So likewise, the phrase, *having been justified,* means someone is doing that act of justification but the immediate context does not tell us who! Theologically, the term, *divine passive* has been recognized. This is not a linguistic category but a theological recognition. We also recognize linguistically that , a verb that is not functioning as a noun or an adjective in the substantive, must have a subject acting on that verb. The recognition here is that when there is no immediate subject acting on the verb then Yahweh or Jehovah

Himself is the subject, hence the recognition of "divine passive."

Yahweh Himself has declared you and I not guilty of all charges. Once a case reaches the United States Supreme court and that court renders a verdict, the losing party cannot appeal to any other court higher and the verdict is final. So when Yahweh declares you and I not guilty then no further appeals can be made to a court or a being higher and we are immediately set free and hence the quotation; *Who will bring a charge against God's elect? it is God who justifies, Romans 8.33.* Someone may rightly pose the question, how then are the elect justified?

The Means of Justification

Now that the question of who justifies has been laid to rest, we can turn our attention to another question; how does Yahweh justify the elect or by what means does He justify? The means of justification may seem to be of less importance to the average church member today but this too is central to the purposes and plan of God for you. The church will rise or fall on this one question. Thomas R Thompson, in his article, "The History of Justification by Faith Alone up to the Reformation", said that, "The doctrine of justification by faith alone may have received notable attention as stated by Martin Luther, but his statement concerning this doctrine is simply an answer to one of the oldest questions that face mankind. That question being, by what means can a person's sins be forgiven? [12]

This question was not an issue for the Roman church prior to the reformation but urgently became the issue that gave birth to Protestantism. This is the one issue that sets in a broader sense, Christianity from all others. We have already established the fact

---

12 https://www.monergism.com/history-justification-faith-alone-reformation

that the act of Justification is entirely an act of God but how then is that act appropriated to the elect?

By faith, it is described in Romans 5:1 as the vehicle by or through which that act of Justification was accomplished. The English word, *by,* that is found in Romans 5:1 has been translated from Greek word*, ek,* and this two letter Greek word has several nuance to its meaning, this word carries with it the idea of ; "to spring or originate from, come from, of the source, out of, of that on which a thing depends or from which it results, of any other kind of origin, from out of, out from, forth from, from."[13] The thrust of this definition is the source, origin and beginning of something.

So then, faith is the source and origin of justification and out of faith, comes justification. Who's faith justifies the elect? Justification did not just happen by or

---

13 https://biblehub.com/thayers/1537.htm

through faith but out of faith. Meaning that faith is not the conduit but origin of it. Someone reading may now be pondering the question but who's faith justifies the elect?. I am happy that you ask and that is certainly a sobering question! This question is also at the center of the election and free will controversy and the thrust of the question is: whose faith saved you? But to answer this question, one must first answer the question, is faith a gift or a work? Is believing God, something that we do or is it a gift from God? The bible actually addresses this issue head on and let's look at a few verses: *For to you it has been granted for Christ's sake, not only to believe in Him, but also to suffer on His behalf,* Philippians 1:29.

For by grace you have been saved through faith; and this is not of yourselves, it is the gift of God, Ephesians 2:8.

Looking unto Jesus, the author and finisher of our faith, Hebrew 12:2.

And I give them eternal life, and they will never perish; and no one will snatch them out of My hand, John 10:28.

These are only a few verses that firmly establish the fact that faith is a gift from God and the reason that you believe God is because He has granted you the faith to believe. So the means or source of our justification is faith and even that faith also is a gift granted only to the elect and so goes the saying that; *those whom He called He also justified,* Romans 8:30. As we have shown by innumerable evidence that the special call of God on the soul of the elect precedes justification but for what purpose did God even bother to justify anyone?

The Result of Your Justification

So why will the God of all the earth elect to justify you and me is a sobering thought to contemplate. Is He not too busy managing the world ? And the thought that He would take time from His very schedule to justify you or me is beyond my comprehension! We have clearly shown that Yahweh Himself performed the act of your justification and faith is the means of justification and even that faith is not ours but a gift from God and the result of that justification is peace with God.

At this point someone reading may raise the question why do we need peace with God because I thought we are always at peace with God? This question hits at the very core of the gospel. Christ Himself said that only those that are sick have need for a physician and I will further add that only those that are sick and know that they are sick have need for a physician. Because many are sick and I mean very sick and do not even know that they are very sick. Of course, Jesus was using a physical situation to illustrate a much deeper spiritual reality.

I would imagine that this is not news to you but again, someone might be hearing this for the very first time that we are by nature, enemies of God and were born enemies of God. The very statement that the result of our justification is peace with God implies that we were not at peace prior to our justification and if we were not at peace then the logical conclusion is that we were at war or enemies of God. Here is what the bible actually says about this matter:

Because the carnal mind is enmity against God: for it is not subject to the law of God, neither indeed can be, Romans 8:7.

You adulteresses, do you not know that friendship with the world is enmity with God? whosoever therefore will be a friend of the world is the enemy of God, James 4:4.

We can clearly discern from these verses that anyone that has not been justified is an enemy of God and the idea of an enemy does not necessarily imply that God hates that person but simply means that you are not yet on His team and from that standpoint, you are an enemy. No one can play on two sports teams at the same time and so you cannot be in the world's team and on God's team at the same time. You will have to love one team and hate the other.

So the result or the goal of justification, being at peace with God, clearly implies that we are by nature, enemies of God and in desperate need of peace with Yahweh. But how does anyone make peace with Yahweh?

The Means of That Result

Any peace making enterprise entails that someone, skilled in negotiation and peacemaking be employed in the process. Someone trusted by the warring factions to bring both parties to the negotiation table. One of the most important peace treaties ever negotiated in the last century, is the

Camp David Accords. These were a pair of political agreements signed by Egyptian president Anwar Sadat and Israeli prime minister Menachem Begin, on September 17th 1978.[14] Jimmy Carter, the United State President at the time, negotiated these agreements between these two bitter enemies. Jimmy Carter was the mediator and the go-between to bring about a peaceful outcome.

So Christ Jesus is our mediator between us and God. Jimmy Carter's peace accord did not accomplish any lasting peace because the parties are still at war as I speak and until there is vertical peace, there can be no horizontal peace. Until there is peace with God, there cannot be any real and lasting peace with fellow humans. The text of scripture says that *we have peace with God through our Lord Jesus Christ* Romans 5:1. The word, "through," establishes the means

---

14 *https://en.wikipedia.org/wiki/Camp_David_Accords*

and medium by which that peace is obtained.

Christ was and is not only our mediator in the likeness of Jimmy Carter but He is the very essence of peace itself. He embodies peace and He is the very personification of peace. *For He Himself is our peace, who has made both one, and has broken the middle wall of separation, having abolished in His flesh the enmity, that is the law of commandments contained in ordinances, so as to create in Himself one new man from the two, thus making peace, and that He might reconcile them both to God in one body through the cross, thereby putting to death the enmity,* Ephesians 2:14-16.

These verses forcefully articulate the fact that God justified you and He Himself performed the act of your justification based on our election, and He Himself is the means and the result of our justification and the end product is peace with God through

His blood shed on the cross of Calvary. Our election is not without controversy as many have questioned the validity of our election and the entire doctrine of election .

Chapter 7

Objections to the Doctrine of Election

The doctrine of election or being chosen by God is arguably the most beloved and hated doctrine in all of scripture. This doctrine cuts into the core of human nature, and that is, our pride and control. Our pride and control is the driving force behind all our thoughts and actions that we will dare not cede control to any being outside of us. The sovereignty of God is also on trial from opponents of election. We will labor to convince our finite minds that we are in control. Imagine , looking down from an aircraft , 38,000 feet or glazing through the window of a ship in the middle of the Pacific ocean, with no trace of land in sight and only then will the thought of powerlessness sink into our feeble minds. So at the heart of any objections to the doctrine of election, is control. Who is in control? Yahweh or I? Those that object to election give several reasons why they find this beloved teaching so reprehensible: God is not fair and shows partiality; No need for evangelization; Election encourages sinful conduct, and let's dive into the details of these objections.

God is not Fair and Shows Partiality:

This objection is by far the most prominent and calls into question several essential attributes of God, namely: Divine sovereignty, Divine foreknowledge, Divine foreordination, Divine mercy and love. The character of Yahweh is called into question by this objection. This objection also exposes the arrogance of humanity. Human pride is fully on display. This is the preeminent of these objections because it cuts into the core of the character of Yahweh

The question of fairness and partiality that is raised by this objection, is also quite interesting because God's scale of appraising fairness and partiality is perfect and no flaw or defect is found in Him. A clear and vivid picture of this is found in the story of the potter and clay and the dialog between God and Jeremiah as God said to Jeremiah; *Arise and go down to the potter's house, and there I will announce My words to you. So I went down to the potter's house, and there he was, making something on the wheel. But the vessel that he was making of clay was spoiled in the hand of the potter; so he remade it into another vessel, as it pleased the potter to make,* Jeremiah 18:2-4.

God used an earthly story of the potter and the clay to teach election, Divine sovereignty , Divine mercy and a host of other attributes of God that are embedded in this story. Notice the instruction from God to go down to "the" potter's house, meaning there was a definite potter and not just any potter and He must have been talking about Himself as the ultimate potter and humanity as the definite clay. Upon arrival, you will see the potter at work making something at the wheel but what he made was spoiled and he made another vessel, as it pleased the potter to make. This is profound, " as it pleased the potter to make." The clay cannot and could not exercise its free will in the hand of the potter. The clay is a passive recipient of the action of potter.

This passivity of the clay is clearly evident in the next interaction between God and Jeremiah, *Am I not able, house of Israel, to deal with you as this potter does? declares the LORD. Behold, like the clay in the potter's hand, so are you in My hand, house of Israel,* Jeremiah 18:6.Wow! this is deep! If my will was free, which I do not believe it is, I would rather take a chance on being completely and totally in God's hands as the potter, than depending on my free will even for a nano second. God's plan of election and His other attributes are clearly evident here above but the phrase, "house of Israel," has given ammunition to some objectors of election.

The phrase, "house of Israel," has been interpreted by some and suggested to say that this passage applies only to national Israel and not to the church or even the gentiles. This view is widely held among dispensationalists, who view national Israel and the church as separate and distinct entities and as a result, they also espouse a two way salvation plan, meaning, one plan for national Israel and another for individual gentiles. But is this truly the case?

The Apostle Paul disagrees with dispensationalists in that he applied

Jeremiah 18 to Romans 9:19-22 in the individual context. Paul clearly taught that salvation for Jew or gentile is always individualistic and not nationalistic. And here is Paul, *You will say to me then, Why does He find fault? for who has resisted His will? On the contrary, who are you, you foolish person, who answers back to God? The molded will not say to the molder, Why did you make me like this , will it? Or does the potter not have a right over the clay, to make from the same lump one vessel for honorable use, and another for common use?*, Romans 9:19-21.

Paul argued that questioning God's fairness or partiality in election is futile and foolish. No one has the ability to thwart the plans and purposes of God. Paul literally calls anyone that makes such arguments, a fool. How can a being (mankind), that is void of any power or ability, question the Being (God), with absolute power and authority about His actions? Paul calls such a person, "a moron". At this point, a skeptic that was sitting on the fence may now be itching to believe in God's plan of election but with one more objection, What is the point of evangelization? Let's be real, any logical person may seem to raise this objection, right? Let's just sit around and fold our arms and be waiting for Christ to return or for the rapture to occur since the elect will be saved no matter what we do, right?

No Need for Evangelization

This objection seems to make a lot of sense on its face value but the assumption that is made by adherents of this objection is that the motivation to evangelize is removed since God has already decided ahead of time, those that He plans to save and they will be saved no matter what action anyone takes. When people lack motivation then it also implies that they are lazy and not inclined to obey the commands of God. This too is far from the truth.

Believing in the doctrine of election is more of the reason to evangelize than not to evangelize. Those that believe in election have had a tremendous impact on the growth of the church for the last over two thousand years. Reformers like John Calvin, Martin Luther, Jonathan Edwards, R.C Sproul , just to name a few. The driving force that proponents for evangelization give is obedience to God's commands and a profound sense of gratitude for the grace of God upon their lives.

Those that believe in election are driven to conduct their lives in complete obedience to God's word and fulfilling the great commission is one area in which they seek to reach the lost. Most adherents of the doctrine of election have a deep sense of calling, purpose and devotion . It is repeatedly said in the gospels, Go into all the world and preach the gospel to every living being. And so, the elect of God will seek to obey this command to the uttermost.

Not only are the elect seeking to obey God as motivation for evangelism but are also fully cognizant of God's method of salvation, meaning, God only saves through His word. Faith is the means but the word is the method of Him saving the elect and here is what he said; *So faith comes by hearing and hearing by the word of God,* Romans 10:17. Paul is asserting in this text that faith comes by some interaction with the holy scriptures. And no one gets saved by observing God's creation, like the skies, seas and all that is in them (general revelation) but by coming face to face with the holy scriptures (special revelation) So then, faith comes by hearing the preached or written word and then the holy spirit works with the word to bring the elect to faith and salvation.

So then Paul will reiterate the point by asking a series of rhetorical questions ; *How then shall they call on whom they have not believed? and how shall they believe in him of whom they have not heard, and how shall they hear without a preacher? And how shall they preach, except they be sent? as it is written; How beautiful are the feet of them that preach the gospel of peace, and bring glad tidings of good things!* Romans 10:14-15.

The elect of God know that their calling is to bring the gospel of peace to the world and knowing fully well that no one will have the faith to believe unless they first hear the word and they will never hear the word unless someone brings the word to them and no one has power to bring the word to them unless God has sent them. The sole duty of the elect is to bring the word to the people and the rest is up to the electing power of God.

You can take a horse to the water but you can never make a horse drink water. The elect can bring people to the word but they can never make the people believe the word. The elect believe wholeheartedly in evangelism and are committed to it but probably not so with most opponents of election who see more problems with this beloved doctrine, accusing it of enabling and encouraging a care-free and sin-filled conduct in daily living. But is this really the case?

Election Encourages Sinful Conduct

The notion that believing in election encourages sinful conduct is also quite interesting. Proponents of this position almost always conclude that believing in election will result in a nonchalant attitude towards daily conduct and the grace of God upon their lives. I was teaching bible study to a small group of about ten students some years ago and one of the women there made a shocking statement that has been engraved in my psychic ever since and here is what she said; “I believe in Jesus and I have gotten my ticket to heaven and I can now go and party and have fun as I want because I got my ticket to heaven.” This woman is certainly of the view that salvation was based on some action that she took, like praying a prayer, joining a church, getting baptized or some other similar human action. Not surprising that this view and attitude are widespread but, it is certainly not a view held by proponents of election.

Adherents of this view are probably not saved at all or under a faulty understanding of election and the doctrine of salvation. A truly saved person that shows evidence of the holy spirit living in them cannot and will not live a life of habitual sinful conduct. Notice that I said, "habitual sinful conduct," and pay attention to what I did not say; I did not say that a truly saved person never sins. The Apostle Paul anticipated that someone or some people would raise this very question and he chose to raise it himself; What shall we say then? Shall we continue in sin so that grace may abound? Romans 6:1.

This is the question in this section, does believing in election lead to sinful conduct? Paul had been speaking about justification by faith in Romans 5:1 and he went on to say; *Moreover the law entered, that the offense might abound. But where sin abounded , grace did much more abound, Romans* 5:20. Paul is making the argument in this verse that the law came to expose sin or offense. There seems to be an increase in sin and lawlessness once the law was instituted but he also argued that when sin increased then grace also increased at faster pace.

So sin could never catch-up to grace because the rate of increase of grace far exceeds that of sin. The growth of grace is exponential in nature and mathematically impossible for sin to catch-up with grace. And so since human beings are very logical creatures, then on the surface, it seems logical for a logical being to infer that in order to get more grace , we ought to sin more, right? This is exactly the question that Paul anticipated and raised, when he said, *What shall we say then? Shall we continue in sin, that grace may abound?* Romans 6:1.

Paul raised this rhetorical question in verse 2 of Romans 6, in which he responded emphatically, " God forbid" or "may it never be". Paul is literally painting a vivid word picture that this kind of thought should never be contemplated by the elect, let alone acting on such a thought. He is stating categorically that the elect of God would and should never harbor this mind set. This objection opens the door for complications that may call into question the security and certainty of any one's salvation.

Chapter 8

Security of the Believer

The doctrine of the security of the believer or eternal security as it is also known, is born out of the question, can a genuinely saved person lose their salvation? Can someone that has been declared righteous by the shed blood of Christ, be declared unrighteous at some future point? This question is very relevant to the title of this book, "Chosen by God," as election itself is at the heart and center. Can someone that claims that Jesus died for them, later in life return to their former manner of life and claim that they had forfeited their salvation for whatever reason?

Eternal Security
in Christ

While I was in seminary some years ago, my Greek professor, Dr Edgar by name, told a story of a student who attended seminary, and was exposed to all the theology, Greek, Aramaic, Hebrew and Latin grammar and graduated with a Master of Divinity degree and at graduation, confessed that he did not believe that Jesus was the Christ. This is someone that went through the rigorous admission process that the admitting committee tries to ascertain that admitted students have made a genuine profession of faith and provide evidence of membership in a bible believing church.

This is a very troubling situation that people come so close to salvation but were never ever genuinely saved. Several studies have shown that millions of people who sit in church pews, sometimes for decades, many even hold church offices like, pastor, deacon, elder, priest and so on, and are ever learning but never able to come to the knowledge of the truth. This section will extensively look at the eternal security of the believer, the assurance of salvation and the extent of the atonement.

Eternal Security of the Believer

The eternal security of the believer is arguably one of the most beloved teachings in all of scripture. It is a dreadful feeling to walk around in constant fear of losing heaven. Some may endeavor to make this a debate over semantics, like debating if the idea of, "eternal security," is even biblical and all I can say is to listen to Jesus's own words on the matter, "*I give them eternal life, and they shall never perish; no one can snatch them out of my hand. My Father, who has given them to me, is greater than all, no one can snatch them out of my Father's hand,* John 10:28-29.

So, how long is eternal life? Is it like ten or one hundred years? Jesus proclaims that He grants the elect, an unending life, life without end and just in case any one doubts what that means, He said it again in unquestionable terms, "and they shall never perish," meaning these that have been granted eternal life shall never again be eternally lost or come into divine condemnation, ever, and they are safe and secure in the arms of Yahweh. And just in case you are still not yet convinced, Jesus hits the final nail on the coffin by reiterating that, "no one can snatch them out of my hand".

It is like keeping your life and my life in the safe of the central bank or the federal reserve bank vault that even the biggest global crime ring cannot gain access to. No one has the ability to snatch them out of My hand. No one has or possesses the ability to violently take the elect or those chosen by God out of the hand of Yahweh, for the elect are under divine lock and key. And just in case some-one out there may raise an objection that these may be some fringe teachings by Jesus and not a central biblical doctrine, then think again!

Jesus was definitely not alone as another writer declares, *To Him who is able to keep you from falling and to present you before His glorious presence without fault and great joy*, Jude 24. This very interesting presentation by Jude combines eternal security and glorification in one verse. The one that possesses the ability to keep and secure you from falling and this is definitely not talking about falling from a tree or hitting your toe against a stone and tumbling head first to the ground. In the context of Jude, he is warning his audience of God's coming judgment on the ungodly from verse 3 through 16 and in verse 17 through 22, he turns his attention to the ones that will not come into condemnation and made a call for their preservation and in the doxology in verse 24 and 25, he reiterated that fact that these will be kept and preserved by God.

These verses say, To Him who possesses the power or ability for the purpose of keeping or preserving you or me from falling from grace or departing from the faith and that is not all, because He will guaranty that you will receive your glorified spiritual bodies and you will spend all eternity in the presence of Christ Himself. And just in case, you are still a skeptic,

Paul raised the bar even higher by making the arguments from the extreme non-possibilities to possibilities, *For I am convinced that neither death nor life, neither angels nor demons, neither things present nor things to come, nor any powers , neither height nor depth, nor anything else in all creation, will be able to separate us from the love of God, Romans* 8:38-39. In my estimation, this is the foremost passage in the entire scripture on eternal security. In these passages, Paul rules out any possibility that someone that Christ died for, could end up in hell or lose their salvation.

In all these passages on eternal security, the Greek word, *dunamos* is used in all three. This word is frequently translated into our English bibles as "can," or "able". The basic idea behind this word is "ability," and Yahweh is the only one with the ability to keep the elect safe and secure. And when this word is used in these passages and many like it, Yahweh is always the subject and the idea that the elect can keep themselves from falling away, hence, lose their salvation, is foreign to the scripture.

Objections to Eternal Security

While eternal security is comforting to many, it is also widely rejected by many in some churches today and through- out the history of the church. The idea of once saved always saved is found to be an affront to opponents of this most comforting and beloved doctrine. Objectors to eternal security, mostly agree that salvation is by grace through faith but they also advocate for a position that salvation can be lost. The argument is made that grace through faith is required to obtain salvation but work is required to keep salvation. How can I work to keep something that I did not work to gain? Remember Newton's third law of motion; For every action, there is an equal and opposite reaction.[15]

If some work or action is exerted to gain salvation then an equal and opposite action must be exerted to keep salvation, And conversely, if no action is exerted to gain salvation then no action can be exerted to keep salvation and therefore, the resultant force is zero. These verses, just mentioned in support of eternal security, are largely ignored or they employ erroneous hermeneutics that deny justice to the plain reading of the text or ignore the context entirely.

---

15 https://www.grc.nasa.gov/www/k-12/airplane/newton3.html

Objectors to eternal security also rely on the scriptures for their objection, and let's look at what Paul said, *Therefore, my beloved, just as you have already obeyed, not as in my presence only, but now much more, in my absence, work out your own salvation with fear and trembling,* Philippians 2:12. The phrase, "work out," has been interpreted by objectors to eternal security to mean that it is up to the individual believer to keep them-selves from falling from grace or losing their salvation but is this what this verse is actually teaching?

I will labor to dive into the linguistics and the context in which this phrase happens to find itself. The Greek word"*katergazesthe"* is where we receive the English translation, "work out your own," and those who emphasize human freedom in matters of salvation have interpreted this phrase to mean exactly what it seems to imply, if taken as a stand-alone text. Thayer's lexicon renders this Greek word as , "to do that which something results, bring about, result in,"[16] This word is in the Greek middle passive form or voice and this simply means that this verb reflects back to the subject. And the subject in this verse is, "beloved."

In a tutorial on New Testament Greek, the author said that, "Remember that voice has to do with the relationship of a verb and its subject. In the active voice, the subject performs the action. In the passive voice, the subject is the recipient of the action."[17] The middle voice reflects the action of the verb back to the subject. An example will be, I am working out salvation, (active voice), I am working out my own salvation, (middle voice), my salvation is being worked out, (passive voice). These examples mostly apply to an English audience because there is some nuance in the Greek middle /passive voice.

---

16 https://biblehub.com/nasec/greek/2716.htm

17 http://ntgreek.net/lesson24.htm

The author of Philippians is telling his audience, (beloved) to work out their own salvation and because the verb, "work out," is in the passive/middle voice and there is no immediate agency attached to the verb then Yahweh Himself is the agent working out your salvation. Yahweh is the one working your salvation and just in case the linguistic argument was not very persuasive to you then we will take a close look at the contextual argument.

Objectors to eternal security often quote this verse in support of their objection but most often do so without properly weighing the context. This verse is not a stand-alone verse without a context. That will be like a tree that stands alone in a very thick forest and that tree is singled out and all other trees are ignored.

After Paul has just finished saying, "work out," your salvation in Philippians 2:12, then this is what he said, *For it is God who is at work in you both to will and do for His good pleasure,* Philippians 2:13. Wow!! Did you hear what Paul just said? This is incredibly amazing! The idea that Philippians 2:12 can be used to defend the potential loss of salvation is not supported by a careful linguistic examination nor the context. If someone was to read only Philippians 2:12, then they would have lost the entire meaning of the text because 2:13 exegetes or explains 2:12. Reading only 2:12 is like reading a verse and stopping in the middle and trying to explain to someone what the verse is talking about. The word, "for", that begins 2:13 explains who is, "working out your salvation," in 2:12. If salvation can be lost as some espouse, then can anyone really be sure of their salvation or sure that they are really saved? I mean, really sure!

The Assurance of Salvation

The assurance of salvation is that subtle inner witness within you that confirms that you are a child of God. *The Spirit Himself testifies with our spirit, that we are children of God,* Romans 8:16. There is an inner testimony between the Spirit (God), and you (elect), constantly confirming your assurance. All that I have just said is only true, if God's Spirit, the Holy Spirit resides in you as Paul said, *But you are not in the flesh, but in the Spirit, if so be that the Spirit of God dwells in you. Now if any man have not the Spirit of Christ, he is none of His,* Romans 8:9.

There can only be an inner testimony, if God's Spirit has taken up residency in your soul. The Spirit can be grieved (Ephesians 4:30) and assurance can be diminished but not extinguished, if the child of God falls into sin. Persistent lack of assurance may be an indication that the Spirit of God is not there and ultimately, that person may not be a child of God. If someone does not genuinely have the Spirit of God living in them , then they cannot have any sense of assurance of salvation.

A few years ago, I had a casual encounter with a friend and an acquaintance of mine and during our conversation, we some-how stumbled on the question of salvation, and he argued passionately that it is impossible for anyone to know for sure that they are saved and are heaven bound. He argued further that anyone who claims to the contrary, is having a false sense of assurance. If someone is not secured then, they cannot be assured of that security either and so assurance is dependent on one's security.

The doctrine of election is front and center to the assurance of salvation and opponents of assurance are often rejecters of several key doctrines, including election. If my salvation and security is ever dependent upon some action that I took, way back when, to accept Christ, join a church, getting baptized, then, I am never going to have any assurance because my security is in my own hands. Once I commit sin then out the door goes my assurance.

But if Yahweh Himself, picked you out of the world for salvation, then He will put His Spirit in you (Ezekiel 36:27) and He confirms that the Spirit is in you by a seal on your life, (Ephesians 4:30) and that Spirit, Who is Yahweh Himself, takes up permanent residence in you, *Who also sealed us and gives us the Spirit in our hearts as a guarantee,* 2 Corinthians 1:22. This text says that the Spirit is given to you as a guarantee and this same Spirit that is given to you is the third person of the trinity.

Whenever you are buying a house and sometimes, a car, you are required to pay a guarantee, pledge or down payment as a way of securing that the entire debt will be paid. That is why, people who buy houses with no money down, easily walk away from their obligations because they paid no down payment and had nothing to lose. The Holy Spirit and God are the same in essence but different in roles and that same Spirit is given to you as a guarantee, a pledge or a down payment that God will come back for the complete redemption of our bodies.

Now, what are the chances that God makes a down payment (Holy Spirit) and fails to show up and complete the deal? If this scenario was a true possibility then salvation can truly be lost? How can someone that Christ died for, end up in hell? This is the crux of the question! Can someone that Christ justified come again under divine condemnation? We had earlier agreed that Justification is to declare a sinner that was formerly guilty and condemned, not guilty and no longer under divine condemnation.

If all this is true then the idea of losing one's salvation, would mean that someone that was declared not guilty by Christ or justified, would have to be re-declared guilty again and come under divine condemnation. Is there any remote possibility of this actually happening? The question being contemplated here is who did Christ die for? What did Christ's death on the cross of Calvary accomplish? This is one of and possibly, the most important question for you to contemplate.

The Extent of the Atonement

The extent of the atonement looks at the reach of Christ's death on the cross. Did the death of Christ on the cross atone for the sins of all human beings or did His death atone for the sins of some only? How far did the death of Christ go in atoning for the sins? At this point, some-one may say, what does the extent of the

Image of the Atonement

Atonement got to do with the subject matter of this book? I will humbly suggest that it has everything to do with the fact that you are elected or chosen by God.

If someone happens to embrace the view that Christ died for the whole world, then they will by default, have difficulty believing in "election", but if they espouse the position that Christ died for the elect, then, believing that you are elected, makes a lot of sense and in-line with the biblical teaching on the subject. I know that at this point, you may exclaim at the top of your voice, "I hate the doctrine of election"! In this section, we will attempt to make an in-depth look into the extent of the atonement and make a compelling biblical case.

Christ died for the World

I did not conduct a scientific survey on this but the view that Christ died for the whole world is by far, the most readily and widely accepted view on the extent of the atonement. Truly, I am hardly astonished by this unscientific survey because this evidently, is the path of least resistance. This is by far, mainstream and any other idea is considered to be on the fringes. It is not surprising, that the way to destruction is a wide path (super highway), and many go in easily but the way to the kingdom is a very narrow way and few find it, (paraphrase of Mathew 7:13-14).

One of the verses that is often cited for universal atonement or Christ dying for the world is, *For God so loved the world that He gave His only begotten son, that whoever believes in Him, shall not perish but have everlasting life*, John 3:16. This is arguably, the most well known and the most quoted verse in the New Testament and possibly, the bible, even by unbelievers. A careless reading of this text may actually seem to say just that, "that Christ died for the world", but wait a minute, really! did He? We will take a keen look at the context of the chapter and the linguistics of the verse itself.

Jesus said to Nicodemus, "unless one is born again, he cannot see the kingdom of God." The meaning of this phrase has to be understood in the context because John 3:16 is in the context of John 3:3. At issue here is the meaning of the word, "again." Everything in John 3:16 hinges on the meaning of this phrase, "unless one is born again." The word "again," found in some of our English bibles, has been translated from the Greek word, *"anothen"*. This word has been translated in several English translations of the bible, like KJV, NKJV,NIV, AMS and NLT as "again," translated by others, like ASV, ERV as "anew" and also translated in some, like CEV, IVS,LSV as "above." This word appears 13 times in the New Testament, [18] and is translated as above or top 11 times and only translated as "again", in John 3:3, 3:7 in some translations and "again," in Galatians 4:9 in almost all translations.

This analysis reveals that this Greek word could be translated as “again”, “anew,” “top” or “above” but the key determinant of its meaning is the context in which it is used. When the relationship of time is in view, then this Greek word is often translated as "again," but when the relationship of location or place is in view, contextually, then it is most likely translated as "above or top." Galatians 4:9 is clearly an example of a relationship of time and the

---

18 https://www.billmounce.com/greek-dictionary/anothen

translators rightly translated the word there as "again," but mostly erred in John 3:3 and 3:7, where relationship of place or location is clearly in view and most well known translations of the bible translated this word as "again".

So the context of John 3:16 is squarely tied to John 3:3, where Jesus told Nicodemus that unless one must be born from heaven or above, he cannot see the kingdom of God. Jesus talked to Nicodemus about the source and location of this birth but Nicodemus understood it to mean the time of this birth. Furthermore, the phrase, "is born again," is also a baseless rendering of the Greek word. It is translated as, "is born again," in several English translations of the bible but the King James Version (KJV), rightly translated this word as, "be born from above."

This sounds like a small thing but not really! it's a big deal because the entire meaning of the text is at stake. The Greek word "*gennethe* ", meaning, "be born,"is in the passive voice, meaning that someone else is the author and subject of your heavenly birth. And since we have a verb without an immediate subject, then it is assumed that God Himself (divine passive) is the subject and author of this heavenly birth. The (KJV), rightly translated this word in the passive voice (be born from above) and the vast majority of English translations, rendered this Greek word as , "is born again," which is in the active voice, meaning, Nicodemus or you are the author of your own birth. So this John 3:3 passage clearly teaches that this birth is heavenly and not an earthly birth. This birth is based on a divine action and not a human action or initiative.

And so the context of John 3:16, that happens to be in the context of John 3:3, must be teaching the same thing. These two phrases in John 3:16 have caused so much consternation over the centuries and the effects thereof are ongoing. The phrases, " For God so loved the world," and "whoever believes in Him." At issue in the former phrase, is the meaning of the word "world," as the object of God's love. Does the love of God truly extend to every human being ever created?

If the word "world" is interpreted to mean global or universal in this context, then the idea that the love of God extends to all humanity, is a clear possibility. But does it? But what does ``world" really mean in this context? Why would anyone end up in hell if Christ's death on the cross extends to all mankind? The Greek word, *"kosmos"*, which has been translated as "world" in our English translations, is described by the Strong's Exhaustive Concordance to have a "broad" or a "narrow" meaning.[19] The broad meaning of the word "world" means all inclusive, universal is readily understood and accepted but the issue is with the

[19] https://biblehub.com/strongs/greek/2889.htm

"narrow" meaning. Here are some examples:

And it came to pass in those days, that there went out a decree from Caesar Augustus that all the world should be taxed, Luke 2:1. Caesar Augustus did not have political control over the universal known world at that time and therefore, lacked the authority and ability to tax all the world. His power and authority to tax was limited to the territories in which he controlled, politically and geographically. Caesar Augustus could only tax the limited world of Caesar. Interestingly, Luke used the phrase, "all the world," and both words, "all" and "world", often seem to imply, universal.

All that the Father gives Me shall come to Me, and the one who comes to Me I will certainly not cast out, John 6:37. The word "all" could not possibly be taken by any serious bible exegete to mean universal. The word "all" in this verse clearly carries a narrow meaning. It is becoming increasingly clearer, even to the utmost staunchest skeptic, that the word , "world" has a narrow meaning and therefore, the extent of the atonement is limited to all that the Father gave to His Son and Christ's death on the cross is limited to the elect and not universal or to the world. He truly died for the world but in the narrow and not the broad sense.

Christ died for the Elect

The very notion that Christ died for some and not for all is an affront to the core human nature. Human pride would raise its ugly head to question the character and nature of God. Putting God's fairness and goodness on trial. The very idea that Christ died for every human being ever born, raises serious theological and philosophical questions. Why would anyone end up in hell, if Christ's dead on that old rugged cross atoned for all their sins? Why would anyone come under divine condemnation after supposedly previously being declared not guilty, acquitted, declared righteous by Christ?

Let's assume that the police officer, Derek Michael Chauvin, who was accused of killing George Floyd in Minneapolis and recently sentenced to twenty two and a half years in jail, was actually found not guilty. Let's say that the jury had actually found him not guilty for killing George Floyd and some other prosecutor decided to bring charges against the same officer for committing the same crime after being declared not guilty in the same jurisdiction. This is exactly what happens when someone claims that Christ's death on that old rugged cross atoned for their sins and yet stands condemned at the final judgment of sinners. No one could be judged twice for committing the same offense. Chrit's death atoned for the sin of Adam in Genesis 3 and that was imputed to all mankind, Romans 5:12 . Adam is our prototype and his sin passed to all humans after him. So Christ only atoned for the sin of those He had chosen once.

In American jurisprudence, there is a doctrine called "double jeopardy" and it is defined as , *A procedural defense (primarily in common law jurisdictions) that prevents an accused person from being tried again on the same or similar charges following an acquittal in the same jurisdiction.*[20] Interestingly, double jeopardy does not have its origin in American jurisprudence but dates back before Christ.

The concept of double jeopardy is one of the oldest in Western civilization. In 355 B.C., Athenian statesman Demosthenes said that the "law forbids the same man to be tried twice on the same issue." The Romans codified this principle in the Digest of

---

20 https://en.wikipedia.org/wiki/Double_jeopardy

Justinian 533 A.D.[21] It is without question that every society in mostly Western civilizations, recognized the need for this question to be codified into law for over 2000 years. And so if corrupt human beings can codify some semblance of fairness in their legal systems then how much more the father of all laws? This will evidently be a clear case of double jeopardy if the blood of Christ atoned for the sin of anyone and that person is brought under divine judgment for the same sin of which Christ atoned for.

The biblical support that Christ died for the elect is overwhelming to the point where there is little comparison. It is like about eighty percent biblical support that Christ atoned for the sin of the elect and something like, twenty percent seeming support for universal atonement or that

---

21 https://www.findlaw.com/criminal/criminal-rights/the-concept-of-double-jeopardy-background.html

Christ died for the whole world. Let's sample a few such support: *Who will bring charges against God's elect? It is God that justifies,* Romans 8:33. Notice what this verse did not say! It did not say, who will bring charges against the world or all?

This verse and many like it, is making known the fact that the sin of the elect is atoned for and they have been justified and declared not guilty and any idea of double jeopardy, is remotely impossible when it comes to the elect. And so that is why it clearly says, *There is therefore now no condemnation to them which are in Christ Jesus,* Romans 8:1. Notice what this did not say! It did not say that, no condemnation to the world but no condemnation to them which are in Christ Jesus. Only those for whom Christ died, meaning the elect, will never come under divine judgment or condemnation.

Just in case you weren't paying attention then please notice the pronoun, "them," meaning that the author was addressing a limited number of people that are guaranteed to be spared divine condemnation. Then, any notion of universal atonement or that Christ died for the whole world is clearly refuted. And just in case you are still sitting on the fence then hear once more, *And shall not God avenge his own elect, which cry day and night unto him, though he bear long with them?*, Luke 18:7. The idea of God's love for the world is very popular but God's particular love is squarely gazed at the elect and no one else. The above text clearly states that God will vindicate His own elect and not the world. That is the object of His love and that is why He will not vindicate the whole world but His own elect. At this juncture, some might say that this isn't fair! What about those who Christ did not atone for their sin? If Christ predestined some to salvation, so what about the rest? did He also predestined the rest to eternal condemnation?

Chapter 9

Double Predestination

Double predestination is the belief that God has from eternity past, predestined some to be saved and to spend eternity with Him in heaven and has simultaneously, predestined the rest or non-elect to hell and eternal condemnation. This is without question, the most despised teaching in all of scripture. Many, even question the validity of this doctrine and may raise questions, like, if this doctrine is even biblical and some would go as far as labeling proponents of this doctrine as heretics. R.C. Sproul called it, "A horrible decree," Most ruthless statement," "A terrible theological theory"[22]

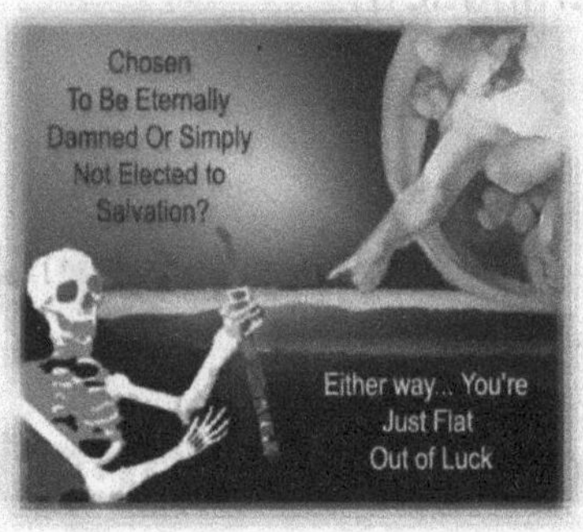

The idea of "double," as inscribed in the phrase "double predestination," comprises two parallel conduits of destinations, and one, a conduit for the elect and the other, a conduit for the non-elect. Both, having their origin from God and one, carrying the elect and headed for heaven and the other, carrying the non-elect and headed for hell. The word, "double" is as opposed to "single predestination," which will carry only the elect to heaven.

---

22 https://www.ligonier.org/learn/articles/double-predestination/

The word, "predestination," comes from two words, "pre," and "destination." I do not intend to bore you with the origin of these words in Greek but the basic idea is that," pre," means before and "destination," as the word itself, clearly implies, meaning, the destiny of the souls of people. The idea behind this is, God, predetermining the future acts and actions of the elect and the reprobate as it regards to exercising or not exercising saving faith in the finished work of Christ on the cross .

While this teaching is embraced by many, it is also widely vehemently opposed and rejected by others. Opponents of double predestination primarily do so on two grounds: They conclude that this teaching contradicts the character of God and it makes God the author of evil by sending people to hell.

This doctrine Contradicts the Character of God

Proponents of this objection, in all likelihood, have an obsession with the goodness of God and almost universally oppose the justice of God. If God is mostly seen and portrayed as a good God , of which He certainly is, and the attribute of His goodness is elevated far above His justice and other attributes of God. The question that is often posed is, Why would a good God send anyone to hell? Sinful man has the audacity and arrogance to question the goodness of God. Here is what the Apostle Paul said, "On the contrary, who are you? You foolish person, who answers back to God? The thing molded will not say to the molder, "why did you make me like this," will it?." Just in case someone out there thinks that this is Paul's idea! hell no! Paul was actually quoting several Old Testament passages like Isaiah, 29:16, 45:9 and 64:8. We are mere mortals and we lack any moral standing to question the motives and intentions of our maker.

The goodness of God goes to the essence and character of God. The core of His being is in His goodness. And here is what He said to Moses about His goodness: *I will cause all my goodness pass before you, and I will proclaim the name of the LORD before you. I will be gracious to whom I will be gracious, and I will have compassion on whom I will have compassion,* Exodus 33:19. Here, God, speaking to Moses, said that I will cause my goodness to pass before you.

We often think of goodness as it refers to God, in descriptive and adjectival terms but here, God describes Himself and His core nature as good. Not merely possessing goodness but having goodness as its core composite structure and as having the absence of evil. And it is out of this that He declared to Moses that *I will be gracious to whom I will be gracious, and I will have compassion on whom I will have compassion.* God is basically telling Moses that "I am God and you are not." He can do as He pleases and no one dares question His character, motives and goodness.

So, it is with utter arrogance that a finite being like man would dare to even contemplate the thought and question: Why would a good God send anybody to hell? Wrong question! The proper question should have been: Why would a just God allow a depraved, corrupt and sinful man into His heaven? Ponder this question and let it sink in and awake your soul from slumber! We have already established that if any one ends up in heaven, it's because God sent them there. But what about those that end up in hell? Can we possibly take God's goodness for granted? certainly not? We know that it is widely believed and expressly stated in the scriptures that God is not the author of evil but what does that really mean?

In the context of double predestination, theologians have gone to great lengths to defend and protect the character of God. I somewhat understand the reasoning behind the defense of God. Any belief that God is the author of evil, makes Him evil but is this really the case? If a Judge sentences a man to be executed, does that make the judge the author of evil since he is the author of the man's death and execution? I guess that there will be hardly anyone who will call into question the character and goodness of this earthly judge but many dare call into question when the judge of all the earth takes action against His creation.

I guess you have heard the phrase: "God does not cause evil but allows evil to occur. " This is a human attempt to protect the nature and character of God. This is for the most part, a philosophical argument as opposed to a theological one. The logic behind this thought process is that if evil proceeds from God, then the logical conclusion is that God is evil. The danger feared by theologians is that Satan is the father of lies and the thought that God is the author of evil will somehow equate Him to Satan. God forbid! Satan can never author anything good because goodness is not in his nature. God is sovereign and Satan is not. God does as He pleases but Satan can only do what God allows but not necessarily approve.

The problem with protecting the character of God is that a lot of killings and calamities in the old testament are directly authored by God. We also have direct and expressed statements from the mouth of God: *The One forming light and creating darkness, causing well-being and creating disaster,* Isaiah 45:7. The Hebrew word "ra", translated here as "disaster", occurs about 667 times in the old testament (BDB lexicon), and this Hebrew word could also be translated as "evil', "calamity", "wicked", "misery", and a lot more synonyms, depending on the context. This is the same word translated as "evil", "knowing good and evil" Gen 3:5, "was only evil continually" Gen 6:5.

Job happened to believe that both good and evil originate from God. *Shall we accept good from God and not adversity?* Job 2:10. The English word rendered here as "adversity," comes from the same Hebrew word "ra". Most translations use the word "adversity" because of the context but the word "evil" could have equally been chosen. The old testament is filled with plagues, natural disasters, wars, killings of individuals and mass killings, all authored by the creator of all the earth. God Himself ordered a lot of these events. There must be a difference between cosmic evil and moral evil. God is incapable of authoring moral evil. God cannot lie, steal, cheat, change, commit sexual immoral acts.

In this sense, God is not the author of evil but a Holy God cannot passively stand-by and allow sin and evil to fester on His earth.

To protect His Holy nature, He is justified in authoring cosmic evil, including sending the non-elect to burn in un-quenching fire. Punishing sin is indeed a loving act. The destruction of Sodom and Gomorrah is one of the clearest examples of cosmic evil authored by God. Here is another action that God took: *Thus says the LORD of hosts, I remember what Amalek did to Israel, how he laid wait for him in the way, when he came up from Egypt.*

Now go and smite Amalek, and utterly destroy all that they have, and spare none of them; but slay both man and woman, infant and suckling, ox and sheep, camel and ass, 1 Sam 15:2-3. The God of all the earth gave a direct command to Saul to go to a city and utterly kill and wipe out anything that has breath, including women and children and was given a stern warning to bring no one alive. God began in verse 2 by giving the reason for His actions. Amalek sinned by ambushing Israel on their exodus from Egypt. God remembered this act years later.

God is clearly the author of cosmic evil and not the author of moral sin but He acted clearly within the bounds of His character and essence and is justified in doing so. Man commits moral evil and God responds by inflicting cosmic evil as punishment. He judges rightly and there is no partiality with Him. He is perfect in His justice and always does what is right. God's ways of dealing with sin are the same across different dispensations and just as He ordered cities destroyed because of sin, He also predestined the non-elect to eternal damnation and un-quenching fire and this too is a loving act but the elect, He predestined to glorification.

Chapter 10

God Glorified You

Glorification is considered to be the final stage of the ordo salutis, (order of salvation), either in the reformed or the Arminian soteriological framework. This understanding of glorification is some-how limited to the protestant segment of the ecclesiastic movement. Glorification is believed to be canonization or something close to it in the Roman catholic or Roman catholic leaning circles. In a wikipedia entry, *Canonization is a decree that the name of the saint be inscribed in Roman Martyrology and that veneration be given to the saint universally within the Church.*[23]

Image of glorification by God

The Roman Catholics do not expressly equate Glorification with Canonization but in essence they do in their practice of veneration. *Veneration is the act by the Church, honoring a saint, and a saint is a person who has been identified as having a high degree of sanctity or holiness.*[24] Adherents of veneration are many, including some sections of Christianity, Judaism,

23 https://en.wikipedia.org/wiki/Glorification
24 https://en.wikipedia.org/wiki/Veneration

Hinduism, Islam and Buddhism.[25] The word veneration comes from the Latin :*veneratio; Greek; "timaw ", "timao"* , mostly translated as to *honor.* This is a human action taken to declare and appraise a deceased person to a state of sinlessness and perfection.

In the reformed tradition, glorification is the final stage of God's redemptive process, in which the redeemed soul attains a state of perfection and ultimate holiness. Two events in the life of the elect would trigger the process of glorification: the physical death of the elect or the rapture of the elect. At the moment of physical death, the soul is immediately transported into the presence of the LORD, (2 Corinthians 5:5) and the body remains on the earth, where it is either buried 6 feet under the earth, cremated, swallowed by some creature or even left to rot in the open field.

---

25 https://en.wikipedia.org/wiki/Veneration

There will be a resurrection of the body, regardless of how the body was buried (Rev 20:13) . God, through Christ will bring the souls of the elect from heaven and raise their bodies from the grave, (1 Thessalonians 4:14-16) and give that resurrected body a new spiritual body (1 Corinthians 15:42-44). The other process that may trigger the glorification process is the rapture of the elect. If the LORD Jesus Christ was to suddenly appear in the clouds today then any elect that has not died physically will immediately be caught up and be violently snatched into the heavens and their bodies will undergo an instantaneous, immediate and radical transformation. Their bodies will not undergo the customary burial but instead a radical change. We will now look at five aspects of glorification: the physical death and or rapture of the elect, destiny of the body, resurrection of the body and the eternal state.

The Physical Death and or Rapture of the Elect

The physical death and or rapture of the elect are events that will actualize and make glorification a reality. There must be a separation of the soul from the body to actualize glorification. *We are confident , I say, and willing rather to be absent from the body and to be present with the Lord,* 2 Corinthians 5:8. The Apostle Paul clearly states in this verse that at the moment that an elect dies, the soul is immediately transported into the presence of the Lord. There is no lapse of time for this transportation of soul to occur but it happens immediately, at the moment of final breath.

Another clearest example of this in terms of the destiny of the soul of the elect is in the case of Lazarus (the beggar)and the rich man. *The time came when the beggar died and the angels carried him to Abraham's bosom. The rich man also died and was buried. In Hades, where he was in torment, he looked up and saw Abraham far away, with Lazarus by his side.* Luke 22-23. This is unarguably the clearest example in all of scripture in regards to the destiny of the soul. This is a case where the body of the elect was buried but the soul was immediately transported into the presence of the Lord. Paul, in 2 Corinthians 5:8 used the phrase "present with the Lord," but Luke used , "Abraham's bosom," and both are speaking of the same location.

Paul only said that the soul appeared in the presence of the Lord but he did not tell us how the soul got there but Luke on the other hand, gave more information about the means of transportation. The angels carried him to Abraham's bosom. After Lazarus breathed his last, the next event on the calendar was glorification. His soul had an angelic transport and escort into the Lord's presence. Even at death ,Lazarus was not alone or lonely but the angels kept him company. Not so with the rich man. His soul had a different destination: namely, Hades. His soul traveled there alone and lonely. No angelic transport or escort and as he arrived, he was welcomed with torment upon torment. But his body, unlike that of the elect, was buried, waiting for the resurrection.

If you are one of God's elect then take comfort in the fact that there is an angelic transport reserved just for you, and that at the moment that you breathe your last, your soul will be immediately transported into the presence of Yahweh. While people are mourning your death as your lifeless body rests in a casket, your soul has already arrived in the presence of Yahweh. *And Stephen said, "Behold, I see the heavens opened, and the son of man standing on the right hand of God." And they stoned Stephen, calling upon God, and saying, "Lord Jesus, receive my spirit",* Acts 7:56 and 59. Stephen definitely had a clear and precise understanding of glorification in that he was beseeching the Lord Jesus to receive his spirit. This is also a case where spirit is used to represent the entire person, as in 2 Corinthians 5:8.

Stephen understood that to be absent from the body is to be present with the Lord. The Lord Jesus is normally sitting at the right hand of the Father but in this rare occasion, Acts 7:56 says that the son of man was standing on the right hand of God. This also tells us that the arrival of the spirit was imminent and immediate and not some distant event. The Lord Jesus would not be standing if the arrival of Stephen's soul was not imminent and immediate. Stephen knew *not to fear them which would kill the body. but not able to kill the soul: but rather fear him which is able to destroy both soul and body in hell*, Matthew 10:28.

Stephen clearly understood and believed that his killers could kill his body but could not harm his soul. His soul was safe and secure in the arms of Yahweh. *And those whom He justified, He also glorified*, Romans 8:30c.

Paul echoed this verse, describing glorification as a past event with future ramifications. What do I mean by that? I am happy you asked! The Greek word that is translated here in the English as glorified, is in the Greek aorist tense. This tense simply means past action. That is why it is translated into English as a past tense. Someone may say, what's the big deal? This is crucial because it has a direct correlation to the fact that you are elected or chosen by God. This means that the action taken by God to glorify you is a past action. In the mind of God, it is done, meaning it has already happened even though you have not yet died physically or be raptured to trigger the actual event.

If you are elected then you are also glorified. You cannot miss glorification if God elected you from the foundation of the world. Here is how Jesus puts it: *For false Christ's and false prophets will rise and show great signs and wonders to deceive, if possible, even the elect,* Matthew 24:24. Jesus is saying here that it is impossible to deceive the elect. Those that He elects must be glorified. They cannot fall by the wayside. The elect cannot be corrupted by false teaching. Now that the soul is glorified, what happens to the body?

Destiny and Resurrection of the Body

After the spirit is separated from the body, (physical death), the body is returned to dust. It matters less how the body is disposed of, but the principle of the body returning to dust is foundational. It makes no difference if death occurred by an aircraft crash, in the sea, by fire, in the forest or the body being missing and was never found. The destiny of the body is the ground and some would dare to ask, why the ground? *By the sweat of your face you shall eat bread, until you return to the ground, because from it you were taken; For you are dust, and to dust you shall return,* Genesis 3:19.

The body represents the likeness of the earth and God made the body from the ground and it is only natural that the body returns to where it came from. The verse above is very explicit on why the body must return to the ground. You must return to a place that has like-essence as you. The reason that we must return to the ground is that we were taken from it. And because our composite DNA make up is dust then it's only logical that our body returns to a place that is like it.

All materials used to build airplanes, cars, buildings, computers, steel and all that our eyes can see are from the ground and will all return to the ground. Speaking of people, Solomon said, All *go to the same place. All came from the dust and all return to the dust,* Ecclesiastes 3:20. This verse gives an exposition on the origin and destiny of the body. The body must return to a place that is like the body. But is there a proper way to bury the body? Does it really matter how the body is returned to the ground? I am happy that you asked!

Traditional Burial VS Cremation

The proper method to dispose of the deceased body is a matter of debate now and has been for a very long time. Traditionally, the deceased body is lowered below the earth and usually, it has been lowered six feet but there has been variations of two to five feet in some instances. In a Wikipedia entry, it says, *excavations vary from a shallow scraping to removal of topsoil to a depth of 6 feet (1.8 meters) or more where a vault or burial chamber is to be constructed. However, most modern graves in the United States are only 4 feet deep as the casket is placed into a concrete box to prevent a sinkhole, to ensure the grave is strong enough to be driven over, and to prevent floating in the instance of a flood.* [26]

This is what I call, below ground traditional burial but there is also what is called above ground traditional burial. This is where the deceased body is placed in a crept space, purchased by the family of the deceased and the crept space is housed in a building called mausoleum, that houses deceased bodies. The below ground traditional burial

---

26 https://en.wikipedia.org/wiki/Grave

has been around since man has been on the earth, while the above ground is a fairly new invention that is seldom found outside of western civilizations. The below ground method has several variations, like mass graves, where several unrelated bodies are buried in a singular grave, then a singular grave, where a single deceased person is lowered alone but what about those who choose cremation as an option to dispose of the body?

Disposing of the Body by Cremation

Cremation is the act of burning the body after it has died.[27] *The box containing the body is placed in the retort and incinerated at a temperature of about 1400 to 2100 degrees Fahrenheit. During the cremation process, the greater portion of the body (especially the organs and other tissues) is vaporized   and oxidized by the intense heat*

[27] https://simple.wikipedia.org/wiki/Cremation

: gasses released are discharged through the exhaust system. The process usually takes 90 minutes to two hours, with larger bodies taking longer.[28] The concept of burning the body has gained popularity in recent memory and some would attribute cost to its rise but on the surface, it looks logical, right?

Some segments of the church and the society at large have believed that cost is the primary reason that families elect cremation for their deceased loved one, but hidden deep beneath the cost issue, is an entrenched belief system about the afterlife. If someone has a shallow or no belief in the resurrection of the body and the eternality of the human soul then such a person will readily embrace cremation as a possible alternative. It is no surprise that cremation is a religious and a cultural phenomena in certain regions of the world. *Indian religions such as Hinduism,*

---

28 https://en.wikipedia.org/wiki/Cremation

Buddhism, Jainism and Sikhism practice cremation.[29]

It is no surprise that all three major world religions, Christianity, Muslim and Judaism mostly disallow cremation as a viable option for disposing of the body except a small segment that has recently been embracing cremation. It is no accident, because all of these three religions contain the old testament Scriptures which are found in our English bible, and are also found in torah and Koran. I can say with some level of certainty that the old testament burial system has greatly influenced the overwhelming rejection of cremation in these three faiths. It is overwhelmingly clear that a belief system, not cost, has a profound influence in someone electing natural burial or cremation.

But, does the bible have anything to say about cremation? I am grateful that

---

29 https://en.wikipedia.org/wiki/Cremation

someone dared to ask! The word cremation is defined as, "the act or custom of burning of the dead," 1620s, from the Latin word *"cremationem"* (nominative" *crematio"*), a noun of action and from the past-participle stem of *cremare* " to burn, consume by fire".[30] There are at least forty seven bible verses of people burned to death or their bodies were set ablaze and here is one which says, *For behold, the day is coming, burning like a furnace; and all the arrogant and every evildoer will be chaff; and the day that is coming will set them ablaze," says the Lord of hosts, "so that it will leave them neither root nor branch.*"Malachi 4:1

This verse was written over two thousand years ago but uses phrases like "burning like a furnace" and "set them ablaze" and this sounds very much like the modern day cremation process, where a body is thrown into an actual furnace and set ablaze. There is no biblical evidence that someone that is

---

30 https://www.etymonline.com/word/cremation

an elect of God was thrown into a furnace and body set ablaze. The only such example is in the book of Daniel, where they were tied and thrown in a blazing furnace and here is how it reads: *Then Nebuchadnezzar was furious with Shadrach, Meshach and Abednego, and his attitude towards them changed. He ordered the furnace heated seven times hotter than usual. And commanded some of the strongest soldiers in his army to tie up Shadrach, Meshach and Abednego and throw them into the blazing furnace, Daniel* 3:19-20.

This is clearly a supernatural event and I can dogmatically say with utmost certainty, that all other occurrences of setting the body ablaze in the old testament, are towards the non elect and symbolizes the fact that those that were set ablaze were under divine judgment. Setting the body ablaze is almost always in the context of divine judgment. And Daniel and his friends were protected from the scorching furnace heat because it was a miracle and they were not under divine judgment and could not be harmed. The natural burial method is clearly supported by the biblical record and history. The body is to be treated with dignity and honor in life and in death. Setting the body ablaze at death is the most dishonoring and despicable act committed against the body.

What someone actually believes about the destiny of the soul has profound ramifications in selecting or rejecting cremation. It is no surprise that religions outside of Christianity, Judaism and Islam, readily and mostly embrace cremation as the favored method of disposing the body. Adherents of faiths that embrace cremation also overwhelmingly embrace annihilation and or reincarnation of the soul . The idea that the soul ceases to exist at physical death as espoused by annihilationists and the idea that the soul returns in some other life forms as espoused by reincarnationists. By believing that the soul is temporal, they seek to cremate the body as a means to wipe out any memory of their existence and eliminate any possibility of ever facing the judgment of God.

No wonder that those of the Christian faith, who embrace the eternality of the soul, overwhelmingly, reject cremation and embrace the traditional burial method. The eternality of the soul and the resurrection of the body are great motivators for embracing the traditional burial system. Some may think that the eternality of the soul is some fringe bible doctrine but it is actually central to the doctrine of election and the entire doctrine of salvation. The bible actually stands or falls on the eternality of the soul doctrine. There are at least one hundred biblical references on the eternality of the soul and to give one such citation: *And do not fear those who kill the body but cannot kill the soul. Rather fear Him who can destroy both soul and body in hel*l, Mathew 10:28.

This one verse is loaded with profound defense for the eternality of the soul. According to this verse, the destiny of the soul is in God's hands alone and even the devil can cause physical death but lacks power and or ability to destroy the soul. The soul does not die or cease to exist and at the moment of physical death. The soul leaves the body and heads to heaven for the elect or heads to a place of silence for the non-elect, waiting for the judgment. The soul can never be annihilated or reincarnated and so, cremation destroys the body but the soul survives intact. Even at cremation, the body is not destroyed in the sense of annihilation or ceases to exist completely because there is a resurrection that awaits all humans who have physically died before Jesus returns regardless of how their bodies were disposed of.

The Resurrection of the Body for the elect

The resurrection of the body physically is the *sine qua non* of Christianity and everything hangs on the fact that there is a resurrection of the body. If the dead do not rise then there is no Christianity and it is just that simple and yet serious. I had about an hour long conversation with a Muslim cleric some years ago and the question of resurrection somehow surfaced during our dialog and for the first time, he came to know that this is a central Christian doctrine. His understanding is that the body of Jesus was stolen by probably His disciples.

According to a Wikipedia entry, most Islamic scholars have vastly varying views on the death of Jesus and here is what it says: *Depending on the interpretation of the following Quranic verses (Qurab=n 4:157-4:158). Islamic scholars and commentators of the Quran have abstracted different opinions and conflicting conclusions regarding the death of Jesus.*[31] These scholars mostly deny Jesus' crucifixion, deny that He died, deny that He was buried. In essence, according to Muslim teachings, Jesus did not rise and there is therefore no resurrection of the body.

Most Jews likewise hold similar beliefs that Jesus did not rise and that His body was likely stolen. Nonetheless, *the resurrection of the dead is a core doctrine of traditional Jewish theology.* [32] This article notes that the Hebrew Bible explicitly mentions the resurrection in the books of Isaiah and Daniel. It is then no surprise that traditional Jews would frown on cremation and embrace the traditional burial as the

---

31

https://en.wikipedia.org/wiki/Islamic_views_on_Jesus%27_death

32

https://www.myjewishlearning.com/article/jewish-resurrection-of-the-dead/

preferred method to dispose of the deceased body. Except a remnant chosen by grace, Jews, by in large, reject Jesus as having come in the flesh and largely reject, practically all the main tenets of the Christian faith, namely: The deity of Christ, the trinity, His full humanity, the virgin birth and it is only natural that they would deny that He rose from the dead. So most Jews embrace the general resurrection of all men but reject the specific resurrection of Jesus Christ.

The resurrection is and remains a mystery and our finite minds are unable and incapable to grasp the mystery of a resurrected body. The Apostle Paul anticipated that his immediate and future audiences would somehow doubt or question the resurrection and then he moved to pose this anticipated question: But someone will say, "How are the dead raised up? And with what body do they come?" 1 Corinthians 15:35. It is pretty logical to anticipate that potentially, someone would raise objections to the idea that the dead will indeed be raised. But anyone with some knowledge of the old testament should have known that the raising of the dead is not some novel Pauline invention but was and is deeply rooted in old testament teachings by the prophets, like Daniel, Isaiah.

Paul responded in an exclamatory tone, by proclaiming that anyone with the slightest inclination to doubt or question the resurrection of the dead is innately, foolish. He calls such a person, *Foolish one* 1 Corinthians 15:36a. This word foolish, comes from the Greek word, "*aphron*" which also means, without reason, senseless, stupid, without reflection or intelligence.[33] Paul is making the case that the resurrection is an oxymoron, complex yet simple and easy to understand. And to drive that point home, Paul makes an

---

[33] https://biblehub.com/thayers/878.htm

agrarian application in which he asserts, *what you sow is not made alive unless it dies*, 1 Corinthians 15:36b. This simple but profound statement will lay the groundwork for his defense that the dead will indeed rise.

Paul's agrarian application emphasizes the fact by observing seed or plant life cycle, which is a clear picture of a resurrected body. If you put a seed into the ground, it must die in order for the seed to bring forth new life. Death is a necessary condition for new life to occur. And moreover, what you plant is not what comes out after the seed dies. When you plant a seed, it comes out with a different kind of body than that which was planted and so is the resurrection of the body.

Now, this idea that death brings newness of life and somewhere, before the seed died, it was living inside a shell and when it germinates, it lives outside the shell and in a different sphere of habitation and so our bodies have to match our sphere of habitation and that is why, *there are also celestial bodies and terrestrial bodies* ! Corinthians 15:40. The atmospheric requirement for earth and that of heaven are different and so a new environment requires a different kind of body.

Terrestrial bodies are those that are adapted and configured for earth and as such, these bodies cannot survive a heavenly environment that is configured for celestial bodies. No wonder, Paul said, *flesh and blood cannot inherit the kingdom of God, nor does corruption inherit incorruption* 1 Corinthians 15:50 . The elect must be given a body that is fit for heaven because a natural body that is made for earth cannot live in heaven. We are not told what would be the genetic makeup of this heavenly body but all we know is that it is not made of dust like the earthly body. It is made of some unknown heavenly material that is not subject to decay and or corruption.

We are also told that this change from one kind of body to another kind of body is instantaneous and sudden with no passage of time. *Behold, I tell you a mystery: we shall not all sleep, but we shall all be changed- . In a moment, in the twinkling of an eye, at the last trumpet, For the trumpet will sound, and the dead will be raised incorruptible, and shall be changed1 Corinthians 15:51-52* . The change from dust to glory will be sudden, instantaneous and miraculous. It will defy every scientific explanation. A body that is subject to illnesses, diseases and death is suddenly radically transformed into an immortal body that does not die ever again, to a hope beyond the grave.

Hope beyond the grave

The doctrine of the resurrection of the elect, has impact, far beyond some theological speculation. This hope is what separates humans from any other being. There is hardly any credible source that gives credible evidence for life after death for any being other than humans. This doctrine has lasting implications far beyond any seminary classroom. When animals or any other living creature dies, their existence, as we know it, has come to an end but not so with humans. Death is not the end unless you happen to espouse annihilationist and or reincarnations beliefs or some other belief system.

Hope is the vehicle which gives humans the reason to wake up each and every morning on this side of life but also for the life that is to come. Without hope, then life is without meaning and purpose. And this hope beyond the grave is not some wishful thinking, that it might happen but a certainty of occurrence and a guarantee of it happening. Sometimes, people would say, "I hope that it rains tomorrow."This is a wishful thinking idea of hope, filled with potentiality and lacking certainty. The biblical idea of hope is a guarantee and not a probability and so this hope beyond the grave is a certain hope.

This hope beyond the grave is not a novel Pauline invention but all the prophets in the old testament looked earnestly to a hope beyond the grave. The most vivid example of human suffering is illustrated in the book of Job and other than the sufferings of Christ on the cross, Job is the other biblical character with tremendous amounts of suffering. Yet, he looked to a life beyond the grave and here is what he said, "*For I know that my redeemer lives, and that he shall stand at the latter day upon the earth*," Job 19:25. Job, speaking under the inspiration of the Holy Spirit, was granted insight into events that are a few thousand years into the future.

Image above of resurrection and ascension

He was granted insight into the fact that his redeemer (Jesus Christ) is alive, and not only that but "He shall stand at the latter day upon the earth". The first part of the verse seems to imply His first coming and the second part seems to imply His second coming and possibly the eternal state, when it talks of standing at a latter day upon the earth. In the midst of Job's suffering, he was given a glimpse of light at the end of the tunnel. In the midst of intense suffering in our own lives, we also can take comfort in the fact that physical death is not the end of our existence. Job began verse 25 by stating, "For I know", implying a very high degree of certainty about events that are probably a few thousand years into the future.

And Job's hope in the midst of suffering was rooted and grounded in his belief in the resurrection of the dead and that the dead do indeed rise. And here are Job's own words, *"And though after my skin worms destroy this body, yet in my flesh shall I see God",* Job 19:26. Job was granted unique insight into the future that hardly any of his contemporaries received. How can Job see God after his skin, worms destroy his body?

Job was permitted by God to see future events that hardly any one in his day was granted such permission. The grave was not his final destination and his body will not remain in the ground even if it rots. I want to make it clear that not all theologians and scholars believe that Job 19:25-26 is speaking of the resurrection but just because the word, "resurrection" is not expressly stated in the passage is irrelevant in my humble estimation. How else would any serious exegete of the biblical text explain Job's words in context?, "And though after my skin worms destroy this body, yet in my flesh shall I see God."

Job clearly was looking forward to a time in the future after he had been dead for a long time and worms destroy his body, which is clearly an inference to his physical death and yet in his flesh, he shall see God. So after he has decayed in the ground for probably centuries, then he suddenly talks about his flesh. How does anyone have flesh from a decayed body? If this is not a resurrected body then someone please tell me what is this? Job must be looking forward to a resurrected body that is going to be completely different from that which was buried and decayed. How can someone who has been dead for centuries have this unshakable hope and confidence of seeing God?

Notice that Job used the word, "shall" in reference to seeing God. He could have said, might or may see God but he said ,"shall" implying a certainty of seeing God. The word hope was not expressly used by Job in this passage but make no mistake that hope was embedded in every fiber of Job's being as he penned down these glorious words. This unshakable confidence kept Job grounded as he endured an unexplainable level of suffering. He kept his eyes toward a future time of peace and tranquility.

There are several other old testament references or inferences concerning the hope beyond the grave but lets now turn our attention to the go-to passage in the entire bible concerning the resurrection and possibility of hope beyond the grave. But before we get into that passage, let's hear one of the most profound questions ever raised concerning hope beyond the grave. This is the question that is on the mind of anyone ever born of a woman. Job had the audacity to raise the question and here is what he asked: *"If a man dies, shall he live again?"* Job 14:14. This question hardly escapes any soul that ever walked the earth. People are hardly concerned about what will happen to their several houses and large bank accounts after they are gone but are primarily concerned with, is there hope beyond the grave?

While working as a chaplain in a local Washington DC hospital several years ago, I visited a patient at the hospital while doing my rounds. The patient must have been in his eighties and had confessed to me earlier that he was an atheist. I entered his room, greeted and handed him a gospel tract that had the caption, "Is this all there is?," and he received it reluctantly and grudgingly but nevertheless, read it completely as I was watching. After he had finished reading, I observed a sudden change in his countenance and he began weeping profusely, covering his face with both hands. I was somewhat taken by surprise and confused and lacking an appropriate response to the situation.

After his sobbing abated, I waited a few minutes and walked away. I perceived that it suddenly dawned on him that his life was about to end and he had no hope beyond the grave. Being an atheist, gave him no hope beyond this life and his life was meaningless and purposeless. If this is all there is then lives are lived in perpetual fear and anxiety of the unknown. This is exactly the situation for billions of people who see no hope beyond this life.

We can now turn our attention to the go-to passage on resurrection in the entire bible. In 1 Corinthians 15:12-19, the apostle Paul made a sequential and logical series of arguments for hope beyond the grave. He began by making an argument from the greater to the lesser. From the resurrection of Jesus Christ to that of the rest of humanity. And here is what he said: *Now if Christ be preached that he rose from the dead, how say some among you that there is no resurrection of the dead?* 1 Corinthians 15:12. Paul is making a statement of fact that Christ rose from the dead. My assumption is that the evidence is so overwhelming that there could be hardly anyone living in Jerusalem who did not know or hear about the front page news when it happened.

Yet, there were rejecters of the resurrection at the time when it happened and was front page news in Jerusalem. Paul said, *how do some of you say that there is no resurrection of the dead?* The apostle Paul's first letter to the church at Corinth, was written about 53-54 A.D and Christ was resurrected about 33A.D. That is about 20 years after Christ rose from the dead. This is very fascinating. Christ was crucified during the feast of Passover, meaning that the population of Jerusalem was probably ten times or more than the normal population without the feast. Every Jew was required to travel to Jerusalem yearly to celebrate the Passover and other feasts but the Passover was the biggest event by far.

The point here is that Christ was not crucified in some little obscure village with only a handful of people present. The people came to celebrate Passover and He Himself was the Passover lamb. And it is without question that He was the center of attention and so His resurrection must have been front page news and yet some say there is no resurrection of the dead. Doubters and conspiracy theorists are not a new phenomenon, for they were there then, and they are here now and they will always be amongst us.

On September 11th 2001, hijackers hijacked three commercial aircrafts, they used one to bring down the world trade center building in New York, the other slammed in the field in Pennsylvanian and the last crashed into the Pentagon building. About three thousand Americans died on a single day. It was broadcasted on live television worldwide for months and yet there are people who doubt that it actually happened. One hundred years from today, no one would probably be alive that was an eyewitness to this horrible event. And it will be debated by historians if this was fact or fiction. And so there were those who were in Jerusalem when Christ rose from the dead yet they say that there is no resurrection.

Interestingly, there are other secular historians who wrote large volumes of history during the time of the resurrection of Jesus Christ. Flavius Josephus was a Jewish historian, who was alive during that time period and mind you that he was not even a Christian and not sympathetic to the Christian cause by any stretch but only provided collaborated eyewitness accounts. Here is what he said: *Now there was about this time Jesus, a wise man, if it be lawful to call him a man; for he was a doer of wonderful works, a teacher of such men as receive the truth with pleasure. He drew over to both many Jews and many Gentiles. He was Christ. And when Pilate, at the suggestion of the principal men amongst us, had condemned him to the cross, those that loved him at first did not forsake him; for he appeared to them alive again the third day; as the divine prophets had foretold these and ten thousand other wonderful things concerning him. And the tribe of Christians, so named from him, are not extinct at this day.* [34]

He affirmed in his writings, antiquities 18:63, quoted above, several key doctrinal issues, including the resurrection from the dead. He also confirmed that *He was a doer of wonderful works.* A clear affirmation of miracles performed by Jesus Christ. Although the original manuscript of Josephus Flavious, was written about sometime between AD 93-94[35] and, yet rejecters cast doubts on some of the language found in antiquities 18:63 by Josephus as an interpolation of the text by Christians. They asserted that Josephus, being a Jew, was affirming core Christian doctrines and they saw that as impossible. Most textual criticism experts and scholars

---

34 http://www.perseus.tufts.edu/hopper/text?doc=Perseus%3Atext%3A1999.01.0146%3Abook%3D18%3Asection%3D63

35 https://en.wikipedia.org/wiki/Josephus_on_Jesus

have found no credible evidence of interpolation and have determined Josephus's manuscripts to be original and genuine.

Now It has occurred to me that rejecters of the resurrection of Jesus Christ, almost always do so on philosophical grounds and not on legal grounds. Philosophical arguments against the resurrection are largely based on reason on the human level. There must be a logical explanation for any action or inaction taken by any being, whether celestial or terrestrial. And such action or inaction that defies reason, would not be entertained. Any result of an action that cannot show a direct correlation between cause and effect, would be immediately rejected. How can a body that was made of dust and has returned to dust through the process of decomposition be reconstructed into a body again?

This would be a clear example of a cause (the body died and has decomposed for about 100 years, more or less does not matter) and the effect (the resurrection from the dead). Since the body was made of soil and has been completely decomposed and became soil and so how is the body reconstructed and separated from soil to become a body again? These questions are based on reason and at the root of these questions, is the denial of the supernatural. Reason and the supernatural or miracles are like mixing water and oil. Oil cannot be intertwined with water, oil can float but cannot be mixed in with water and so is reason and the supernatural. The supernatural and reason are a bed of strange fellows and a case concerning the resurrection cannot be prosecuted based on reason but on legal grounds.

I will humbly submit to you that the case concerning the resurrection of Jesus Christ can only be prosecuted on legal grounds and not on philosophical considerations. Let's say that in a hypothetical case, John Doe is charged with the killing of his wife, Susan Doe. It has been several months and the body has not been found. Prosecutors are charged with the duty to provide physical evidence like a dead body, a gun, knife or some other weapon, blood samples, blood soaked clothes, blood in a vehicle. Eye witness account, like who saw it happen and how many people saw it and are they credible. A family member or a friend to the accused may not be considered credible. Circumstantial evidence is evidence that may infer that a crime has been committed. This will be like why did John Doe take one week to report to the police that his wife was missing?

With all the evidence in the world presented by the prosecution, John Doe could manage to make a philosophical argument even if the body is discovered after about seven months and has been decomposed . John Doe could possibly argue that just because he has not heard from his wife does not imply that she is not alive. He may even try to discredit any eyewitness account as not credible and even proceeds to discredit the credibility of the eyewitnesses. And even when faced with the evidence of a dead decomposed body, he may come up with something, like, the body is too decomposed to ascertain the real identity of the deceased. He may even move to discredit the autopsy report by discrediting the credentials and expertise of those performing the autopsy.

Any philosophical arguments advanced by John Doe shall fall short in determining his innocence. The resurrection of Jesus Christ can only be prosecuted on the human level on legal grounds . It has to be based on physical evidence, eye witness account and circumstantial evidence. Lets first of all look at physical evidence. If this was to be presented in a court of law today, the evidence is overwhelming. Let's look at the legal case for the resurrection of Jesus Christ through the lenses of physical evidence, eyewitness accounts and circumstantial evidence.

Physical Evidence For the Resurrection

Now first we will look at the physical evidence: The stone to the entrance of the tomb was rolled away, Mark 16:4. Mark describes the stone as, "very large", Mark 16:4. Mathew gave us more information about who rolled the stone away: A severe earthquake had occurred and the angel of the Lord came from heaven

and rolled the stone away, Mathew 28:2. There were also Roman guards guarding the tomb as it is said, *the guards shocked for fear of him and became like dead men, Mathew* 28:4. When news got to Simon Peter and the other disciples that the Lord had risen, they immediately ran to the tomb for physical verification. And upon arrival, Simon first entered the tomb John 20:5 and another physical evidence is presented, "the linen wrappings lying there," and the face-cloth which had been on His head, John 20:7. And the location of the wrappings and face-cloth was different, John 20:7.

The tomb was empty as it is recorded, *but when they entered, they did not find the body of the Lord Jesus,* Luke 24:3. Another dilemma is on the horizon; and now that the tomb is empty, so where is the body? News came that He is risen but where is He? The Angel of the Lord made this announcement to the women who were at the tomb, He is not here, for He is risen, Mathew 28:5. Jesus met his disciples , the women and all who were waiting to see Him in Galilee, Matthew 28:7-9. But John actually records that the women actually met a man at the tomb but not knowing that he was Jesus and they thought that he was a gardener, John 20:15. Thomas put his finger and verified the wounds on his side, John 20:27.

Now, the physical evidence is overwhelming but that alone may not be enough to sway the staunchest of skeptics and conspiracy theorists of the resurrection and so we turn our attention to eyewitness accounts and see if we can make head-way in chipping away doubts.

Eyewitness Accounts to the Resurrection

The resurrection was not some secluded private matter but was in every sense of the word, a public affair. It happened during Passover and Jerusalem was bustling with people and activities. Unless someone just came from another planet, like Mars or something like that, then the death, burial and resurrection of Jesus was on the mind of everyone in Jerusalem. Listen to this conversation between Jesus and two individuals immediately after His resurrection, on their way to a village, named, Emmaus:

And behold, on that day two of them were going to a village named Emmaus, which was sixty stadia from Jerusalem. And they talked with each other about all these things which had taken place. And while they were talking and discussing. Jesus Himself approached and began traveling with them. But their eyes were kept from recognizing Him. And He said to them, "what are these words that you are exchanging with one another as you are walking?" And they came to a stop, looking sad. One of them, named Cleopas, answered and said to Him, "Are you possibly the only one living near Jerusalem who does not know about the things that happened here in these days? And He said to them, "What sort of things?" Luke 24-13-19.

This text is a clear indication that the resurrection of Jesus Christ was no secret and could not have possibly been a secret. This was the talk of the day in every conversation. Cleopas is asking Jesus (not knowing that it was Jesus at the time) , something like, where have you been? Are you the only one near Jerusalem, not to have heard the news? He appeared to Mary and she saw Him, she called Him "Rabboni" meaning, Teacher, John 20:16. Mary Magdalene testified to the disciples that "I have seen the Lord." He appeared to the disciples, in-spite of a shut door, John 20:19. He appeared to Thomas alone, John 20:24. There was the testimony of Joanna, Mary the mother of James, also other women with them testifying to the apostles.

He appeared to the eleven and those who were with them, Luke 24:33. We are not told how many people were with the disciples, but there were an untold number of witnesses, whose identity was not revealed. He was seen by about five hundred brethren at once, 1 Corinthians 15:6. Legal arguments for the resurrection of Jesus Christ are overwhelming and the physical evidence and eyewitness accounts presented thus far is enough to sway even the staunchest of skeptics. But it is understandable that there are those who, for what-ever reason, cannot be moved by any amount of physical evidence or eyewitness accounts (unless they are the elect). Can any amount of evidence sway you if you are still a skeptic after reading this far? Maybe circumstantial evidence!

Circumstantial Evidence for the Resurrection

Circumstantial evidence is evidence that comes through inference or to substantiate a fact through inference. In any legal argument, the weight of the case hangs on physical evidence. Even eyewitness accounts can sometimes have counter eyewitnesses but physical evidence is the most difficult to refute. No wonder that those who would deny the resurrection of Jesus Christ, schemed to put in place a plan to refute any physical evidence presented, (namely, the resurrected body). They knew clearly that they could debate eyewitness accounts but would handily lose any debate with a resurrected body staring them in their faces.

Now while they were on their way, some of the guards came into the city and reported to the chief priests all that had happened. And when they had assembled with the elders and consulted together, they gave a large sum of money to the soldiers, and said, You are to say, His disciples came by night and stole Him away while we were asleep. And if this should come to the governor's ears, we will win him over and keep you out of trouble. And they took the money and did as they had been instructed;

and this story was widely spread among the Jews, and is to this day Mathew 28:11-15.

So why would the Chief Priests and the elders go to such great length to refute the resurrection? They were fully aware that He is risen because it was the most talked-about event at the time. There were primarily three groups of Jews at that time: the Pharisees, Sadducees and Essence . The Pharisees believed in the immortality of the soul and the resurrection of the body and the afterlife; the Sadducees believed in the mortality of the soul, that the soul ceases to exist at the moment of death and no physical resurrection of the body; [36] And the Essence is really not mentioned in the bible under the same name and it is commonly agreed that they are no longer in existence. And so we will limit our observation to the Pharisees and Sadducees. The Sadducees were the more powerful elite. Most in the

---

36 https://www.gotquestions.org/Sadducees-Pharisees.html

Sanhedrin were Sadducees and did not believe in the resurrection.

And so it makes perfect sense that any physical evidence that runs counter to what they believe must be squashed. No amount of physical evidence would persuade a Sadducee to accept the resurrection. The chief priests and elders were most certainly Sadducees or they were those in the majority with decision making power. The Romans ran the political side of Israel and the Jews, mostly, the Sadducees were in control of the religious side. They had to come up with a credible response to the circumstantial evidence, (empty tomb). Everyone knows that dead people do not suddenly walk out of the grave and so they saw this as the only possible way to explain away the empty tomb.

The fact that Jesus was crucified was hardly a big deal to the Sadducees because crucifixion was a pretty common method to punish criminals and the fact that He died was also not a big deal to them, people die daily, since Adam. But that He rose is a big deal and they cannot accept that. They also took steps to conceal another circumstantial evidence: The missing guards or soldiers who were tasked with guarding the tomb of Jesus. The text does not tell us the exact number of guards or soldiers that were assigned to this very important mission but I can infer that they were many because of the importance of the mission and the text refers to them as "soldiers" in Matthew 28:12, meaning more than one.

We know that the guards at the tomb of Jesus were Roman officers, under the control of the then Roman Governor, Pilate, but the governor had placed them at the disposal of the Jewish authorities. They had asked Pilate to give the order that the tomb should be secured until the third day. They reminded Pilate, what Jesus had said when He was alive, that He will rise again on the third day. And so Pilate granted their request to make the tomb as secure as they know how, Mathew 27:62-65.

Rome had a very strict military disciplinary code for misconduct and most of the punishments for misconduct were punishable by stoning to death. And so losing a prisoner that is under the control of a Roman guard is a very serious matter. Losing the body of Jesus that was placed under Roman guard was likely to receive the same punishment as losing a prisoner. So the idea suggested to the Roman soldiers by the Sadducees that the body of Jesus was stolen by His disciples while they were asleep does not fit the character of a Roman soldier. A Roman soldier does not have the luxury of falling asleep while on duty. This is another attempt by the Sadducees to explain away any circumstantial evidence. How can the body in a well guarded and fortified tomb be missing?

What about the large stone placed at the entrance to the tomb? The stone is described as being "extremely large," Mark 16:3, and some have suggested that the stone could weigh as much as half a ton. There is so far no clear archeological evidence as to the weight and size of this stone but all we know is that it was an "extremely large" stone. This is also circumstantial evidence that leads to the empty tomb. The Sadducees did address how and who removed the stone. The idea that this stone was extremely large is not far-fetched because it required supernatural activity for the stone's removal. There was a severe earthquake, requiring the movement of earth.

There was angelic action and activity. The angel of the Lord left heaven and descended to earth just to roll the stone away. The reaction of the on-lookers, being the Roman guards, was shock and awe. They became as dead men, Matthew

28:2-4. This also is circumstantial evidence that enhances the case for the resurrection and a certain hope beyond the grave. And I hope that I have made a compelling case that there is indeed a resurrection and Christ was raised from the dead. Paul will continue to make several compelling reasons and consequences if there was no resurrection at all.

But if there is no resurrection of the dead, then is Christ not risen, 1 Corinthians 15:13 . Paul is making a link between the general resurrection of the entire human race to the special or specific resurrection of Jesus Christ. Many in his immediate audience were fully aware and believed that Christ rose from the dead and Paul is making the case that, since that is true for Him then it will be true also for the human race. And if the dead do not rise then Christ has not risen. Most of the people know full well that Christ is risen and that must also be true for the human race . Then he proceeds to make an interesting connection between the resurrection, preaching and faith. And if Christ be not risen, then is our preaching vain, and your faith is also vain, 1 Corinthians 15:14.

Paul is making the case that without the resurrection of Christ, then it is useless preaching and also useless believing. The point is that preaching and believing cannot exist without the resurrection. The resurrection is the central ingredient to preaching and faith or believing. The Greek word *"kenos"* has been translated in this verse as "vain", in the verse above but, this word could also be translated as *void, empty, without effect, no purpose, fruitless, labor acts which result in nothing.* [37] The point is that time is being wasted in preaching and believing if the dead do not rise. And the after effect of that will be false

---

[37] Thayer's Greek: 2756. κενός (kenos) -- empty (biblehub.com)

testimony of something that never happened.

Yes, and we are found false witnesses of God; because we testified of God that he raised up Christ: whom he raised not up, if so be that the dead rise not, 1 Corinthians 15: 15. Being found to be false witnesses of God is a very serious matter. Paul had been preaching from village to village and testifying that God had raised Christ from the dead and exhorting people to put their faith in Christ for salvation. Paul is making the point that if Christ had not risen then he would be considered a false witness for giving false testimony about Christ. This is very serious because Deuteronomy 19:15-21 prescribes severe penalties for anyone accused and found guilty of being a false witness or giving false testimony. This is not a risk that Paul would want to take, knowing the grave consequences that await him.

For if the dead rise not, then is not Christ raised: And if Christ be not raised, your faith is vain; you are yet in your sins, 1 Corinthians 15:16-17. This is the climax of Paul's argument. The centrality of the resurrection in Christ's redemptive work. If He died and stayed in the grave then the rest of humanity will also die and stay in the grave. That is why Paul said that your faith is worthless, empty and void. The bottom-line is that sin cannot be atoned-for without a firm belief in the resurrection . The phrase, "you are yet in your sins" means that there has been no change in your status and you are still in your sinful state and your faith in Christ was a waste of time if Christ was still in the grave and never rose from the dead.

No one goes to heaven without believing in the resurrection. And the result will be that all who had died, assuming that there was no resurrection then their existence had ended. And here is what the text said, *Then they also who have fallen asleep in Christ are perished*, 1 Corinthians 15:18. Verse 17 is making the case that if Christ be not raised then you are yet in your sin, meaning that you are not saved and verse 18 states that even those that have died thinking that they were saved, have perished, meaning, they are in hell because without the resurrection, any such believe, was in vain.

If there is no hope beyond the grave, then life has no meaning, value or purpose. Most people that chose to commit suicide are dealing with a lack of purpose and meaning in life. They do not see their lives as having any value and meaning and they chose to end their existence on planet earth. And not because they want to die, but they have lost the desire and hope to live. This is the apostle Paul's take on the matter, *If in this life only we have hope in Christ, we are of all men most miserable*, 1 Corinthian 15:19. Interestingly, millions of people put their hope in Christ to protect them from illnesses, get them a good job, grow their business, find a good marriage partner, give food to eat, protection from accidents and all other human wants and needs that feed the human imagination.

Notice that the text says , "if in this life only we have hope," and the word "only" or alone is used to qualify a singular focus and attention given to one thing. Paul is not saying that hope in Christ in this life is unimportant and that it should be ignored but he is emphasizing the fact that it should not be our main and only focus. And as a matter of fact, the life to come should occupy our time on this side. We are on this side, only for about one hundred years at the most, but on the other side, for eternity and so shouldn't it be logical that more of our hope and focus should be on the life beyond the grave? That should certainly be our hope, not on things that are perishable but on things that are imperishable. Paul refers to the elect as "aliens", on the earth Philippians 3:20, whose citizenship is of the heavenly realm. But yet those without this hope are also waiting for a sure resurrection of the body.

Resurrection for the non-elect or non-chosen

Is there really any hope beyond the grave for the non-elect? Let's just make it real: So let's say that your loved-one, family, friend or acquaintance has just died and you attended the funeral and finally, the deceased body is lowered into the ground, cremated or whatever means the family chose to dispose of the body. What is going through your mind about what has happened to them as you take the long and lonely walk going home, assuming that you knew that they were not a follower of Jesus? Is that really the end of their existence? In this section, we will seek to address the destiny of the soul, the body and final resting place for the non-elect.

The Destiny of the Soul of the non-elect or non-chosen

The bible has a lot to say about the soul . The soul is described as the immaterial part of humans and at other times, described as the material part of humans. The human make-up consists of body and soul and sometimes the entire human is addressed as "soul". The soul that sins shall die, Ezekiel 18:20. This verse calls the entire person, "the soul". In the creation account it says, *And the Lord God formed man out of the dust of the ground, and breathed into his nostrils the breath of life and man became a living soul,* Genesis 2:7.

And so prior to the body becoming a living soul, it was just a lifeless body and a pile of dust on the ground. And so "the breath of God" into the pile of dust of the ground, established a new entity, called, "a living soul." And so the dust of the ground plus the breath of God equals a living soul.

Interestingly, the word, translated in most of our English translations as "soul" is translated from the Hebrew word *Nephesh* and this word could also be translated as "living being, person, self," [38] depending on the context. We often think of soul as an immaterial and separate non tangible part of man but this verse addresses the entire person, including the body, as soul.

This adjective "living" in this verse also qualifies the soul as "living soul." The implication of this qualifying adjective, "living" could be the immortality of this new entity called, "soul." Man is composed of the dust of the ground, the breath of God, which is also the spirit side of man and the result is the soul. Even though the soul, often represents the whole person, it also at other times represents the non-material of man and at other times humans are referred to as having body, soul and spirit, 1 Thessalonians 5:23, but several other verses

---

[38] https://biblehub.com/bdb/5315.htm

referred to humans as having two parts, body and soul or body and spirit, Ecclesiastes 12:7, Mathew 10:28, and at other times, it refers to the whole person as soul, Luke 1:46-47, Mathew 16:26.

The spirit also has two components to it: the spirit, (meaning human spirit) which every human being possesses, Genesis 2:7 and the Holy Spirit, which only the elect receive at the moment of justification, Romans 8:9. Rachel's soul departed from her body, Genesis 35:18, signifying her physical death. And we have definitively established the fact that the soul and or spirit are distinct from the body and the soul departs from the body at the moment of physical death but where does it go to for the non-elect?

There are lots of speculations about the destiny of the souls of the non-elect at the instant and moment of physical death, when the soul separates and departs from the body. One of the clearest insights into this question is found in the story of the rich man and Lazarus. And it reads, *Now it happened that the poor man died and was carried away by the angels to Abraham's arms; and the rich man died and was buried. And in Hades he raised his eyes, being in torment, and saw Abraham far away and Lazarus in his arms. And he cried out and said, Father Abraham, have mercy on me and send Lazarus, so that he may dip the tip of his finger in water and cool off my tongue, for I am in agony in this flame*, Luke 16:22-24.

At the moment that the non-elect dies, the body is disposed-of, by whatever means that the family chooses, traditional burial, cremation or whatever but his or her soul, immediately appears in a location, called, "Hades". The text says that, "and in Hades he raised his eyes, being in torment," establishing that fact that "Hades" is a real location and not some fictional or imaginary place as many would want to believe. The body is laid to rest but the soul is alive, alert and cognizant of its location and environment. The soul is not asleep or soul-sleeping but alive.

The text says that, " he raised his eyes," meaning, it was alert, it can perceive and think. It has feelings because the text says that, "being in torment," meaning, the feeling of pain did not cease at death for the non-elect. Memory of events of past life was not lost at death. The body has decayed in dust of the earth but memories of this life are not lost at death. They are carried and stored in the soul. The text says that, (speaking of the rich man) "and saw Abraham far away and Lazarus in his arms." He did not forget events in this life. This makes a very strong case for the immortality of the soul. He recognized Abraham and Lazarus from a distance and instantly knew who Lazarus was and how he lingered outside his gate and ate the trash out of his garbage.

At the end of verse 22, the rich man said, "for I am in agony in this flame." The rich man did not cease to be a person just because he died and his soul was in Hades. Personhood is maintained in the soul and not in the body and it is therefore no surprise that the soul is more often used as a synonym for the complete person. Your true DNA is in your soul and not in your body. Humans are fascinated by what we can see, touch, feel, smell but show with little or no fascination with the soul. The soul cannot be seen, touched, felt or smelt and so its importance is neglected and ignored. The rich man was not passive in his pain and no pain killers would have relieved his agony. He felt the full weight of his agony. He even asked for Abraham to send Lazarus to bring some water to cool off his tongue. So the rich man is now in a place called Hades but where is that exactly?

The exact location of Hades is a matter of debate as some would even espouse the view that such a place does not even exist. But before taking a critical look at a place called "Hades", I will present a few facts about this place. This word, Hades, is translated in the old testament from the Hebrew word, "Sheol," and refers to a place where the dead go, (Psalms 88:3 and 5). This same Hebrew word can equally be translated in our English translations as grave, hell, pit, underworld and abode of the dead. Remember this very important rule in biblical hermeneutics or the science of bible interpretation: words alone mean little or nothing, absolutely, without a context. The meaning of any word must be drawn from the context. The old testament uses the word, "Sheol," sometimes, depending on the context, to mean "grave," in the general sense for anyone that has died, wicked or righteous. And here is an example; *"If I wait for the grave as my house, If I make my bed in the darkness,"* Job 17:13.

Job here was speaking about ,"wait for the grave," and that is the same word "Sheol," and we know that Job's soul is in heaven but his body is in the grave awaiting the resurrection and not in a place of torment like hell or Hades. The New King James Version of the bible (KJ), NLT, rightly translated the Hebrew word, "Sheol" as grave but other translations, like the New American Standard Bible and many others, transported the Hebrew word, "Sheol" into the English translation. They are technically accurate but that leaves the average English reader a little confused, especially if they have been thought to believe that the word "Sheol," always means Hades or Hell and is a place and destiny for the non-elect at death and a place of darkness.

And here is another text that makes the point clearer: *For you will not abandon my soul to Sheol; You will not allow Your Holy One to undergo decay*, Psalms 16:10. And this same verse is quoted in Acts 2:27 as a fulfillment. This word, "Sheol" is translated in Acts 2:27 as Hades and it is definitely not talking about the unregenerate going to eternal condemnation but is actually, fulfilled in Christ Himself as this is a messianic Psalm. It is safe to conclude that Sheol could be used in the general sense to mean, grave for anyone who dies regardless of their standing with God, but is also widely used to refer to a place of utter darkness, where the unregenerate go, waiting to be cast into the lake of fire.

Here is one such description of this dreadful place: *Sheol below is excited about you, to meet you when you come; It stirs the spirits of the dead for you, all the leaders of the earth; it raises all the kings of the nations from their thrones,* Isaiah 14:9. Sheol is planning and preparing a welcome party for the souls of the non-elect to arrive there.

This verse identifies the location of Sheol as below and in this verse, Sheol embodies a person that welcomes the arriving souls of the unregenerate as they arrive at their transition point waiting to be cast into the lake of fire.

Also to note that the souls of the elect are already in heaven but souls of the non-elect are in this place of torment, located in the underworld, called Sheol or Hades. The final destination of the souls of the non-elect is the Lake of fire and here is what John said; *The sea gave up the dead that were in them, and death and Hades gave up the dead that were in them, and each person was judged according to what they had done. Then death and Hades were thrown into the lake of fire. The lake of fire is the second death.* Revelation 20:13-14.

We have argued all along that at the moment of physical death, the soul of the non-elect immediately transitions to a place called Sheol or Hades but the above text says that , "the sea gave up the dead that were in it, and death and Hades gave up the dead that were in them." That means that these are locations for the dead: sea, death and Hades. Do these locations have bodies or souls in them? These were most likely resurrected bodies because they had to be judged as said at the end of verse 13 before being cast into the lake . And after the judgment, only death and Hades are thrown into the lake of fire.

There is much speculation as to the meaning of "death and Hades were thrown into the lake of fire." We have argued that the destiny and location of souls after physical death is Hades or Sheol but in this verse death is mentioned as a location for the dead prior to being cast into the lake of fire. What is this all about? I want to believe that "death", in this passage, represents the non-elect that were physically alive but spiritually dead and did not die physically prior to this judgment period. They transition from being physically alive, then judged and cast into the lake of fire. And those in Hades represent the non-elect that have physically died and were in Hades or Sheol and also being judged prior to being cast into the lake of fire. Not everyone believes that at the moment of death, the souls of the non-elect arrive in a place called Sheol or Hades.

Some believe that there is a place called Purgatory that holds the souls of the dead in transition but does such a place really exist? and who goes there? Purgatory is defined as an intermediate state after physical death for expiatory purification. The word , "purgatory," (in Latin *"purgatorium")*, a place of cleansing, from the verb *"purgo"*, (Latin) "to clean, cleanse", as a noun, it appeared perhaps only between 1160 and 1180, giving rise to the idea of purgatory as a place.[39]

---

39 https://en.wikipedia.org/wiki/Purgatory

Purgatory is widely believed today to be associated with Catholicism but its history has its roots into antiquity. And here is the Roman Catholics take on purgatory: *The Roman Catholic doctrine of purgatory teaches that people who die in God's grace but who are not sufficiently purified of their sinfulness to enter God's presence must undergo a time of purification through temporary suffering the torments of purgatory. Unlike hell, purgatory is not a final judgment on the wicked but rather a finite period of purging for the insufficiently righteous.*[40]

The Roman Catholic doctrine asserts that those "who die in God's grace," and this phrase leaves many including me, baffled and wondering, what do they mean by "who die in God's grace." To die in God's grace would probably mean, saved in the

40 https://carm.org/roman-catholicism/purgatory-and-2-maccabees-1239-45

protestant mind set but difficult to discern what it really means in the Roman Catholic mind set. The next phrase is quite interesting as it asserts that, "but who are not sufficiently purified of their sinfulness to enter God's presence." How can anyone die in God's grace and at the same time, found not to be sufficiently purified? Who then determines the correct amount of purification required to enter heaven? Who then is the gatekeeper? They continue to identify purgatory as a place of "finite period of purging for the insufficiently righteous." Is there anyone sufficiently righteous to enter heaven? Whose righteousness are they inferring? The last time that I checked, our righteousness is as filthy rags.

This finite period is not yet determined and it does not tell us who determines the length of this finite period. The doctrine of purgatory leaves a lot more questions than answers. These doctrines are contrary to the biblical doctrine of election. Salvation and redemption is entirely an act and work of Christ alone and no human action can and will place anyone into heaven. Christ's shed blood on that rugged cross is the only means by which a sinful man or woman gets a right standing before a holy God. Justification is by faith alone through Christ alone, because without the shedding of blood, there is no forgiveness of sin (Hebrews 9:22).

In a Wikipedia entry, the author asserts that, *Perhaps under the influence of Hellenistic thought, the intermediate state entered Jewish religious thought in the last centuries B.C.E. In Maccabees we find the practice of praying for the dead with a view to their after- life purification. The same practice appears in other traditions, such as the medieval Chinese Buddhist practice of making offerings on behalf of the dead, who are said to suffer numerous trials. Among other reasons, Catholic teaching of purgatory is based on the pre-Christian (Judaic) practice of prayers for the dead.*[41]

This Wikipedia entry is making the point that the purgatorial doctrine is not new and predates the New testament era. And this has even influenced Jewish religious thought and several other cultures in the old testament era. I can conclude with a very high degree of certainty that the root and likely origin of the intermediate state, called purgatory, is found in the prayers for the dead in 2 Maccabees 12:42-45. The conclusion must have been made that if this book exhorts its readers to pray for the dead then the assumption is made that there must be some hope after death but before heaven. Hence the origin of a place, called purgatory. This is the prayer that has brought so much consternation over several centuries: *And they begged him that this sin be completely blotted out. Then Judas, that great man, urged the people to keep away*

41 https://en.wikipedia.org/wiki/History_of_purgatory

from sin, because they had seen for themselves what had happened to those men who had sinned.

He took up a collection from all his men, totaling about four pounds of silver, and sent it to Jerusalem to provide for a sin offering. Judas did this noble thing because he believed in the resurrection of the dead. If he had not believed that the dead would be raised, it would have been foolish and useless to pray for them. In his firm and devout conviction that all of God's faithful people would receive a wonderful reward, Judas made provision for a sin offering to set free from their sin those who had died 2 Maccabees 12:42-45.

Atoning for sin or transgression always involves an individual action and blood is always the means for a sin offering, or for the covering or removal of transgression in the old testament, but in 2 Maccabees 12:4:43, Judas Maccabeus takes a monetary collection from his men to send to Jerusalem to provide for a sin offering. The reason for the collection is stated in the next line that says that, "because he (Judas Maccabeus) believed in the resurrection of the dead." The implication here is that the sin offering was being offered for those that had died and not those that are living. And the collection of money was used to purchase the sin offering. The atoning of sin by means of blood sacrifice is the central message of the entire old and new testament.

There is no redemption or forgiveness of sin without blood sacrifice. *For the life of the flesh is in the blood, and I have given it for you on the altar to make atonement for your souls, for it is the blood that makes atonement by life*, Leviticus 17:11. This is the pivotal tenet of Protestantism. This one issue sets Protestantism apart from all other faiths. I was once speaking to a Muslim cleric and I asked to explain to me how a sinful person gets into right standing with God? And he responded by saying, man has to do good deeds and at the end, God will weigh if the good outweighs the bad. So I ask him, how good does one have to get and how can anyone know that they have crossed the finish-line?

And his response was, "no one can know for certain". I told him that blood must be sacrificed for sin to be removed and he responded by saying, "that was not necessary". All the old testament animal blood sacrifices were shadows or pointers to the real and ultimate sacrifice that was to come. This is how John the Baptist introduces Jesus, the ultimate sacrificial lamb: *The next day he saw Jesus coming toward him, and said, Behold, the Lamb of God who takes away the sin of the world!* John 1:29. John the Baptist is stating in this verse that all the old testament sacrificial systems were pointing to the ultimate sacrifice of Jesus on the cross of Calvary.

So the idea of collecting money for sin offering for those that have died as mentioned in 2 Maccabees 12 is an anathema to the gospel. Praying for those that have died is also a strange and novel idea advanced by text in 2 Maccabees. And the reason advanced for praying for the dead is the belief by Judas Maccabeus in resurrection. The assumption that is made for offering prayers for the dead is that there is some hope after physical death for repentance but is that really the case? The implication here is that there is no consequence for sinful behavior while someone is alive. Any idea that someone would repent in the grave or some place between death and heaven, is pure fiction at best.

Here is what Jesus told His audience: *Therefore I said to you that you will die in your sins; for unless you believe that I am He, you will die in your sins,* John 8:24. This is the core teaching in Protestantism, there is no repentance in the grave and no need to pray for the soul of a deceased person. At the moment of physical death, their eternal destiny is settled and no sacrifice for sin or prayers can alter that destiny. Prayers and sacrifices are made for the physically alive and spiritually dead persons because the book of Hebrews tells us that, *And just as it is destined for people to die once, and after this comes judgment,* Hebrew 9:27. If a person dies without Christ or not saved then the next event on their calendar is judgment, before being thrown into the lake of fire. No need to give people a false hope where there is no hope.

The author of 2 Maccabees is not identified but in a Wikipedia entry, it is identified as a fellow named Jason of Cyrene, a Hellenistic Jew who lived around 100 B.C, as the possible author. This book was rejected to be included in the protestant canon for several reasons, including failing to pass the test of canonicity. All old testament books of the bible were authored by well known prophets in Israel or a King, like King David, who wrote most of the Psalms. It also contradicts the rest of the protestant bible on several doctrinal issues, and most notably, "praying for the dead." This book is embraced by the Roman Catholics and several orthodox denominations and it is included in their canon. The Catholic bible contains 73 books and the protestant bible contains 66 books, excluding 2 Maccabees. Praying for the dead is a doctrine vehemently, rejected by the protestant wing of Christianity.

The Roman Catholics on the other hand embrace praying for the dead souls that they believe are in a place called purgatory. And if they are in limbo or a place of transition then there must be some mechanism to transition them out of there. In the system in 2 Maccabees 12:42-45, the living persons took up collection of money for sin offering for deceased persons.

Interesting similarity between the Roman Catholic system and early Jewish system. The Roman Catholics system did not offer sacrifice for sin but did something identical. They introduced a system called indulgences.

Indulgences

An indulgence, *from the Latin:" indulgentia " from the verb "indulgeo" , translated as permit, is a way to reduce the amount of punishment one has to undergo for sin. The Catechism of the Catholic Church describes indulgences as "a remission before God of the temporal punishment due to sins whose guilt have already been forgiven."*[42] The basic idea behind an indulgence is for the living to perform some action on behalf of the dead whose souls are located in a place called purgatory, to obtain their release. The Catechism of the Catholic Church, describes an indulgence as remission before God of

[42] https://en.wikipedia.org/wiki/Indulgence

sins whose guilt has already been forgiven. This statement is filled with theological contradiction and nonsense.

How can sin whose guilt has already been forgiven, require remission again? This is total nonsense. Once sin is forgiven by God, it is done, so long as justification is concerned. At the moment that a soul is justified, that soul also is granted immediate and instantaneous forgiveness from God, that soul is also converted. There is no forgiveness in the grave. Indulgences require that its recipients, do something, perform some action to earn indulgences, which will gain the release of someone else from purgatory.

In a Wikipedia entry, the author said, *The recipient of an indulgence must perform an action to receive it. This is most often done by saying (once or many times) a specific prayer, but may also include the visiting of a particular place, or the performance of some specific good works.* [43] So repeating some specific prayer , visiting some particular place as prescribed by the Roman Church or doing some specific good work as also prescribed by the Church will gain someone an indulgence. The Roman Catholic is the sole arbiter of who is in purgatory and who gets an indulgence. The power to determine someone's eternal destiny according to this system is within the Church. The result of that power was that indulgences rapidly became a money making machine for the Church. I mean, let's be real! So you are told that someone that you love so dearly has died and their soul is in a place called purgatory and all you have to do is pay an amount of money to get them out of limbo and into heaven.

And if you believe that to be the truth and you have the resources to act then what is going to stop you? Nothing, I guess! We are told that *By late middle Ages, indulgences*

---

[43] https://en.wikipedia.org/wiki/Indulgence

were used to support charities for the public good, including hospitals. However, the abuse of indulgences, mainly through commercialization, had become a serious problem which the church recognized but was unable to restrain it effectively. [44] The sales of indulgences was the catalyst that gave birth to the Protestant Reformation. If not for this one issue, the Protestant churches that we have today may not be in existence. This issue caused a revolt within the Roman Catholic Church that resulted in the beginning of Protestantism.

The Protestant revolt caused so much tumult within the Roman Catholic Church that they had to defend the doctrine of indulgences. They were forced to redefine the purpose and meaning of indulgences. They even tried to walk-back the idea that indulgences secured forgiveness of sin and a release from purgatory. Because of their inability to scripturally provide an apology

[44] https://en.wikipedia.org/wiki/Indulgence

for the doctrine of indulgences, most Roman Catholic theologians would argue publicly, that indulgences do not provide forgiveness of sin or a release from purgatory but in practice, indulgences are firmly entrenched as a core Roman Catholic doctrine. At issue with this doctrine, is the doctrine of salvation. By what means does a sinful and corrupt human being get into a right standing with his or her creator? Plainly put in lay man's terms: by what means does anyone get saved?

This is a question of the means of justification. People fought and died for this. Those who dared to oppose the Roman Catholic teachings were excommunicated and many died by execution. Are humans saved through faith alone and through Christ alone or are humans saved through a performance and works based system designed by man and controlled by the Church? The phrase, "in Christ alone through faith alone," was coined during the reformation and around 1517 AD. It is pretty clear, scripturally, that justification is entirely a work of God that puts the sinner in a position of peace with God (Romans 5:1) and that is accomplished through faith that God grants the sinner (Ephesians 2:8-10). No human effort will get anyone into heaven.

If there is a place called purgatory then there must be a way to get those souls out of there. Remember that these are the souls of deceased persons and are in a lifeless state. These deceased souls are unable to perform any action that would change their location because they are deceased. Remember Newton's First Law of Motion, which states that a body at rest will remain at rest unless an outside force acts on it. This law was intended for physics and mechanical engineering but it certainly applies to our context. Dead bodies or souls don't move unless some force outside of them moves them. The basic idea behind indulgences is that someone alive, like a family member, friend or priest, takes some action as prescribed by the Roman Catholic church for the purpose of affecting the movement of the deceased soul from purgatory to possibly, heaven.

Catholicism and Hell

There is no clear agreement for the destiny of the souls that leave purgatory onto their final destination. Where do they really go? Do they all go into heaven or do some go to hell? A glimpse into the answer to this question takes a look into the doctrine of sin through the lenses of Catholicism. The doctrine of sin is foundational and all other doctrines stand or fall based on the understanding of doctrine of sin. If someone's doctrinal position on sin is faulty then there is a high likelihood that they will be wrong on several other doctrines. Thomas Aquinas, a well respected Catholic theologian had this to say concerning hell:

Hell is reserved for the wicked and the un-baptized immediately after death, but that those who die only in original sin will not suffer in hell.[45]

This quote lays the groundwork for several other doctrines like purgatory and indulgences. The baptism that is referred to in his quote is clearly, water baptism and he is making the assertion that anyone that is not water baptized is going to hell. That makes salvation a human action and something that the Church can control. He also asserts that those who die in original sin will not suffer in hell. This is a very serious theological error that I cannot fully refute in the limited space allotted to me in this very small book.

The original sin that he is referring to, is what happened in Genesis 3, when the entire human race fell and was separated from God. Those who die in original sin will

---

45 https://en.wikipedia.org/wiki/Thomas_Aquinas

actually suffer in hell but he is asserting the contrary. This is a way to get people to go through purgatory so that the Church can sell more indulgences to get them out. Nonetheless, hell is a real place that the non-elect will occupy. The elect will not but will be raised with an immortal body that is decay free and this immortal body must live in an environment that is free from disease and decay, hence the new heaven and new earth.

The Eternal State

The eternal state is a phrase coined by theologians to represent the coming new environment called the new heaven and the new earth. Since this environment is free from defect and imperfection, its occupants must also be free from defect and imperfection. The eternal state will have no hospitals and doctors, because sicknesses will be eradicated. No more pain medication because pain will be done away with. No funeral homes and burial grounds because the people will live perpetually and death will be eradicated. And no more sorrow because Christ will wipe the tears from every eye. This new heaven and earth is new in essence and quality. This new environment is different in several ways:

No Memory of Past Human Habitation

This new environment has no resemblance of the past. The previous topography had soil, rivers, oceans and all other living things that occupy the earth. *See, I will create a new heavens and a new earth. The former things will not be remembered, nor will they come to mind,* Isaiah 65:17. Since the body and soul have been radically transformed, the new environment must also be changed to match the bodies and souls of its new residents. The occupants will have no memory of earth or ever lived on earth. *Having the glory of God. Her light was like a most precious stone, like Jasper stone, clear crystal*, Rev 21:11. There is no modern city on the earth with anything that closely resembles the new Jerusalem. These gold like materials are made to paint a picture of what it is like but there is no likeness of it on the earth.

No Negative Emotions

Have you contemplated the fact that there will be no negative emotions in the eternal state? Why would anyone want to miss such a place is beyond my comprehension and the simple truth is that many may not find themselves there. Many are searching for happy times in this life when it can only be found in the life to come. This is how God puts it, *But be ye glad and rejoice forever in that which I create, behold, I create Jerusalem a rejoicing and her people a joy. And I will rejoice in Jerusalem, and joy in my people: and the voice of weeping shall be no more heard in her, nor the voice of crying,*

Isaiah 65:18-19. This is the place to be! everlasting joy and not a single sad face ever.

We are not able to exhaust the splendor of the eternal state in this brief study but there is nothing in its likeness on this side of life. Peace will be perfected as the lion and lamb will sit inside a McDonald's and feast on a cheeseburger. No wars or rumors of wars! No disobedience! for the elect or those chosen by God will obey all the Lord's commands perfectly.

Conclusion

The biblical doctrine of election or being chosen by God and the fact that you are elected to be on God's team is unarguably the most humbling teaching in all of scripture. At the core of the doctrine of election, is man's or human's complete inability to elect or choose a holy God for salvation. Man, in his natural state, lacks the desire, power or ability to exercise their free will in choosing a holy God . The human will is not really free but is completely and wholly in bondage and bound to sin. The human will is dead, like a dead corpse. That is why Jesus so eloquently said in John 8:36 that "if the Son sets you free, you are free indeed".

The assumption that can be inferred from Jesus's statement in this verse is that humans are naturally bound and in bondage to sin. Those whom the Son sets free, are those whom he foreknows, meaning, God had determined beforehand to establish a love relationship with those that He also predestined to be conformed to the image of His son. Those that He has elected or chose are also those that He especially called, regenerated and justified.

Some may ask the question: How do or can I know that I am an elect or have been chosen by God? That is a fair question! The simple answer is that no one except God knows those whom He has elected or chosen. But a number of events must happen in the life of the one chosen by God, except or unless the elect dies as an infant or is saved at the moment of final breath, like one of the thieves on the cross. Here are some points to watch for in the life of the elect:

1) The elect loves God's word and is burdened with an intense desire to know His word and do His will. They are also

burdened to know what God has said in His word.

2) The elect are very sensitive to sin and walk in obedience to God and His word.

3) The elect are burdened with reaching the lost for Christ. They are on mission with God.

4) The elect are peacemakers. They will actively seek forgiveness and carry the burden of how they have been forgiven by Christ's death on the cross.

5) The elect experiences a deep inner peace as the Spirit of God witnesses with their Spirit that they are the children of God.

6) There is an intense hatred for sin in the life of the elect.

7) There is an intense burden in the life of the elect to live a holy life.

If these things are true in your life and abound then in all likelihood, you are already one of God's elect. If you find yourself suddenly gaining interest in God's word and your desire to study His word is exponentially increasing, then maybe, God is drawing you to Himself and you are potentially one of His elect. And as your faith grows, and you do His will, abstain from sin, there will be an inner confirmation within your spirit that you are indeed one of His chosen. And if not then all hope is not lost so you are alive, keep praying seeking His face.

The doctrine of election, while beloved by many, is also passionately opposed by others. At the heart of that opposition, is the character of God. His justice is often called into question. His goodness is often elevated above His justice. The question that is often raised is, "why would a good God send anyone to hell?", And the question that I would often ask is, "why would a just God allow anyone into His holy heaven?" Rejecters of election also espouse freedom of the human will. They argue that the human will is free and not in bondage.

When I ponder the depth, breadth and height of the simple truth that the God of all the earth would contemplate and consider to elect such a wretch like me, then I would suddenly burst into tears and weep uncontrollably. Always carrying this burden within me and constantly asking the question! Why Lord? Why me Lord? I come to grips with my own inadequacies and unworthiness. I am always reminded of the saying, " For consider your calling, not many wise according to the flesh, not many powerful , not many noble. But God has chosen the foolish in the world to put to shame the wise." (paraphrase of 1 Corinthians 1:26-27).

The joy of being chosen by the creator of the universe is inexpressible and God's love for the elect or His chosen one's is inexhaustible. If you are one of God's elect or has been picked out from the crowd and chosen by God, then know and be assured that you are safe and secure in His arms and no one is able to snatch you out of His hands. Not even death shall separate you from Him. . If God has chosen or elected you then rest assured that you will soon be seated with Him and never to be forsaken by Him. Put your trust in Him. He will certainly glorify you, Amen and Amen.

About the Author

Waltere Asili Koti is the author of several books, including, "Fending off Suicidal thoughts," "You are Elected," "Understanding and Overcoming your Emotional Issues," "Understanding your Emotions," and recently, "The Power of Sex."

Waltere earned his master of divinity degree (MDiv) in theology from Capital Bible Seminary in Lanham Maryland and was completing his doctor of theology (ThD) degree from Faith Theological Seminary in Baltimore Maryland. He also completed several years of clinical pastoral education and practical training at several hospitals, including, the VA Medical Center in Hampton VA,

Washington Adventist Hospital in Tacoma Park MD and Washington County Hospital in Hagerstown MD. He is a board certified clinical chaplain and a board certified pastoral counselor. He worked as a clinical chaplain at Washington Adventist Hospital in Tacoma Park, MD.

He has counseled thousands dealing with all kinds of spiritual and emotional issues, like aloneness, loneliness, fear, anxiety, depression, sexual addictions, addictions in general, marital issues and even suicidal ideation.

He lives in the Baltimore area with his wife and family.

Reviews Request

We are very grateful that you have purchased a copy of this book and have labored tirelessly to read it. We hope and pray that you have gained valuable and life transforming insight. If this book has touched and impacted your life in any way, then we will appreciate it, if you will be so kind as to let others know, by leaving a review for us on Amazon, Barnes & Nobles, Goodreads, Google.

If you were looking for somewhere to eat and you found two restaurants, one with zero reviews and the other has fifty five stars reviews, where would you go to eat? Your review is very important to us.

Thank you very much for taking the time to leave a review.

www.ingramcontent.com/pod-product-compliance
Lightning Source LLC
Chambersburg PA
CBHW011833020426
42335CB00024B/2846